Curiouser & curiouser

By the same author

Little princes (Sidgwick & Jackson, 1981)

Curiouser
&
Curiouser

the best of
Sue Arnold

Constable London

This collection first published
in Great Britain 1985
by Constable and Company Limited
10 Orange Street London WC2H 7EG
Copyright © Sue Arnold 1985
Set in Linotron Plantin 11pt by
Rowland Phototypesetting Limited
Bury St Edmunds, Suffolk
Printed in Great Britain by
St Edmundsbury Press
Bury St Edmunds, Suffolk

British Library CIP data
Arnold, Sue
Curiouser and curiouser: the best of Sue Arnold
I. Title
082   PR6051.R62/

ISBN 0 09 466660 1

For Edward and Joanna
(who are in the same hole)

Contents

Contents

Rural Rides

Foreign Parts

Introduction

I have no illusions. I am a jobber, a hack, honed to deliver a specific number of words by a certain time for an agreed wage. And why not? It keeps the bairns in shoe-leather and their mother off the streets. In this breezy spirit I offer these trifles for your attention. If you prefer snacks to six-course blow-outs, sonatas to opera, Twiggy to Tessie O'Shea, then I think you will like them. Enjoy them as you would a soufflé, a glimpse of a meadowful of poppies from a speeding train.

Some day, of course, I shall deliver up my *Oeuvre*, my epic, my 800-page modern classic, each sentence chiselled to slip effortlessly into every finely wrought paragraph; but for the moment I dip and peck and perch, content to remain a sprinter, for to be honest I have neither breath nor inclination for the cross-country run.

I daresay it's because until I joined the *Observer* I had a pretty sketchy upbringing. I went to ten schools, dipping in and out of different education systems as my parents moved house or took up jobs abroad. When I was seven my father joined the Bombay Burmah Trading Company in Borneo, and my mother decided to join him. These were the frugal post-rationing '50s when international companies did not, as they do now, subsidise school fees and air fares, and when my mother said good-bye to me at the convent of St Francis de Sales in Tring, it was to be a two-year separation. It was not so much the prospect of losing my parents as the fact that the nun who opened the convent door had a black moustache that made me sob, stick my fingers in my mouth and start gnawing my nails down to the knuckle, a habit that I retain to this day.

I don't remember much about the following two years except that I collected twenty-two sets of rosary beads and every month a parcel arrived from Sarawak containing two dozen bars of chocolate and a tin of Mackintosh's toffees from my parents, which for a day or two made me the most popular girl in school. I needed the monthly boost. Being half Burmese in those days wasn't, as it is now, considered exciting or exotic. I grew used to being called Chinky and asked why my eyes went up at the sides.

My mother returned from Borneo; she had remarried and we moved to Hampshire and bought a small farm. It was mainly pigs and chickens with a few sheep thrown in. I remember when the first three sows arrived, the first to set foot in our soil was called Lady Luck, and thereafter all the pigs had Burmese names to please my sentimental Burmese mother: Ma Nya (Miss Night), Ma Chit (Miss Love), Ma Hla (Miss Pretty), Ma Shouk (Miss Busybody). Joe the pigman, whom my mother had head-hunted from Liphook station where he worked as a taxi driver, couldn't be doing with all this Oriental whimsy. He rattled the bucket of pig nuts, shouting, 'C'mon Daisy, Peg; Lily, Gert, good girls.'

I was by now at my eighth school, a posh private boarding-school with a pair of joint headmistresses, forerunners of Hinge and Bracket. It was at this time, egged on by the local dancing-school mistress, that I acquired my theatrical vocation and coerced my parents into sending me to a stage school. I was thirteen, podgy (particularly about the thigh thanks to my previous vocation – to be the next Pat Smythe), but I was determined to see my name in lights. For the next three years I became a dedicated Terpsichore, learning every conceivable permutation of la dance from Cecchetti to Busby Berkeley, tap, folk, character, national, highland and soubrette. I wasn't much good. Being small and different-looking, I was invariably cast as the jester or the cat or the saucy knave who gets his ears boxed in end-of-term productions. I was also far too self-conscious to thrive on stage. While classmates simpered and pouted and made eyes at the audience, I shrank and blushed and felt ridiculous. My mother tried to console me. 'Don't worry darling. Who wants to be shameless? And anyway, you'll grow out of it.' Fortunately my stage career was nipped in the bud. At fifteen I was expelled for insubordination and limped off to the nearest technical college to pick up some academic padding.

I don't regret my abortive stage career, I made some good friends. Some of them became Bluebell Girls at the Lido in Paris. Others too small for such honours (five foot ten inches was the minimum for a Bluebell in those days, half of it leg) joined dance companies playing panto in the winter and end-of-the-pier summer shows. Years later I ran into a former stage-school chum in Iran. I was there on a story and she was dancing with a travelling company at a nightclub called the Shoukafay Noo in downtown Teheran. Her name was Diana Bishop. She was a vicar's daughter from Dorset, and a less likely Middle Eastern cabaret artist you'd be pushed to find. At school in St Luke's dorm she had cried herself to sleep because she missed her family and the vicarage.

'What's it like here?' I asked when I went backstage after the show. It was the usual glamorous behind-the-scenes set-up: half-naked girls removing their make-up, drinking Nescafé from plastic cups and washing out their tights in cold water.

'This isn't too bad,' she said. 'At least we don't have to consummate like we did in Istanbul.'

'What do you mean, consummate?' I said nervously.

'Go out after the show and chat up the customers to make them buy us champagne and teddy bears,' she said. 'Don't look so worried, nothing else.'

After technical college, Trinity College Dublin to read English, with a sabbatical year at the University of Colorado. I had no particular feeling for Whitman or Twain, but four years in the same place seemed too long for a pecker-and-percher. I didn't care for America, largely because the Americans didn't care for me or at least they didn't understand me. How could someone who passed for Puerto Rican in New York, Chinese in San Francisco, Navajo Indian in Montana and Mexican in San Antonio speak with an English accent? My hybrid ancestry had its advantages, though. Hitch-hiking round the North American continent with a girlfriend, I ran out of money and got a job in an art gallery in Chinatown, San Francisco because, said the proprietor, Mr Fung, he trusted me. It wasn't until a week later I found out the gallery was a front for a porn shop.

In my last year at TCD (these were the halcyon days when there were still jobs to go to) I wavered between a career in advertising, industry, the British Council or maybe even journalism. I went in for a competition sponsored by J. Walter Thompson to find the ten most ingenious under-graduates in Great Britain – the prize for each being fifty quid and a job as a trainee copywriter. I emerged the seventh most ingenious undergraduate in Great Britain, took the money but refused the job. Instead, I played safe and sensible and went for a final interview with ICI for a posting in Dyestuffs at Slough. There were six of us going through the 'are they officer material?' course. The other five made it. I tried a week as a supply teacher in East Ham, where for some mysterious reason I supervised sewing classes, and that put me off teaching and the British Council.

So that left journalism. Away I went to Blackburn as a cub reporter on the *Evening Telegraph*. It lasted six months. I was the only unmarried female over twenty in the town, and my social life was indifferent. The high point of my week was to go to the Mecca ballroom at lunch-time on Wednesdays with

Marilyn the switchboard operator, and there we would twist and shout in unison for an hour, eat a cold mutton pie at the Bull, and return to the office. Sometimes boys would come up and ask one of us to dance. 'No thanks,' we'd say. 'Can't you see I'm with my friend?'

I moved south and got a job as a holiday relief on the London *Evening Standard*, only to be booted out by the Union for not having completed my provincial indentures. I drifted to the London office of the *Manchester Evening News*, where I wrote about knitwear and delivered purple prose for their 'Down Memory Lane' feature about the Crystal Palace fire and the sinking of the *Titanic*. I drifted onwards to the *Daily Sketch* gossip column, surely the tattiest job in Fleet Street, and got the sack after three months for getting the bride's name wrong at a society wedding at St Margaret's, Westminster.

I returned cap in hand to J. Walter Thompson. 'Remember me? I was your seventh most ingenious undergraduate last year and you offered me a job? I've decided to take it after all.'

'Fine,' they said, 'but you'll have to take another test.'

For three hours, this was worse than finals, I sat in a pokey room overlooking Berkeley Square, answering questions like 'Write a jingle for a new doggy breath-freshener,' or 'Explain in not more than twenty words how to make toast, to a visitor from outer space,' or 'Draw a picture epitomising humility.' I handed it in. 'Sorry,' said the J. Walter Thompson creative boys. 'You seem to have lost all your ingenuity in the last twelve months. Have you thought about retail?'

Washed up at twenty-two. I got a temporary job demonstrating how to shrink-wrap tins of cat food in a Piccadilly shop window with a pretty BOAC air-hostess called Ginny who'd been grounded with a phantom pregnancy. We wrapped cat food by day, and by night we drank pink gins with travelling sales reps from the Midlands who had seen us at work in our see-through orange overalls as they strolled to Green Park.

It was then that I met a certain ageing American jazz impresario who spent three days in L.A. organising concerts for Ella Fitzgerald and Duke Ellington, two days in Lucerne sorting out his divorce, and two days in London for the culture. And for me.

The details of this sporadic mid-week relationship I shall reserve for that 800-page epic, though as a rule of thumb I would advise every young woman at some stage of her life to befriend a millionaire. Suffice it to say that when the attachment ended my friend – no, let us not mince words, my sugar daddy – sent me, by way of a farewell present, a single first-class ticket to Teheran.

'Why Teheran, for Heaven's sake?' I asked the girl at the Hilton Hotel travel agent who telephoned with the information.

'Well,' she said, 'what he actually said was Timbuctoo, but the connections aren't great so I booked Teheran instead. It's about the same distance.'

Thus it was that I found myself working on the *Teheran Journal*, an English-language daily read by the 90,000 Europeans and Americans who lived in this booming pre-Ayatollah capital. I visited Isfahan, Persepolis and the Caspian Sea, and learned for the first time what censorship meant. Every morning an official from the Ministry of Information came to proof-read our copy. Certain words were forbidden. There were, for instance, no slums in Teheran (the newspaper office itself was situated in an area of indescribable squalor). Nor could we write the word 'student', for students in those days of the American-subsidised Peacock Throne were synonymous with revolutionaries. They were right to be wary.

Teheran was always a temporary posting. I still hankered after Fleet Street, and returned with a fistful of job-application letters which I sent out on a weekly basis. Three months later I was offered a job for two weeks as a holiday relief on the Pendennis column of the *Observer*, and by dint of luck and low cunning managed to stay on making myself, if not exactly indispensable, then at least useful. There followed four years on Pendennis, a stint on the news desk, and eight years ago a weekly spot in the magazine.

So much for the history, now for the high tech. The two questions I get asked most often are: Where do you get your ideas? and How do you get to write a column? The first is simple. From *anywhere*. From eavesdropping on buses, from talking to people in lifts, from PR handouts, from readers, and more often than not from other people's waste-paper baskets. The Great Chain of Creation goes something like this. An idea for a story is sent to the news desk. *Nothing in it for news, try features* scribbles the news editor in one corner, and passes it on. Features diverts it to the women's page, who reckon it has a City page slant. The City boys asset-strip it and recycle it to Pendennis. When there is hardly any more space for re-addressing, someone scrawls *Try Sue Arnold* across the top, and eureka, I'm in business.

As for the qualifications – well, you could do worse than have a degree, a diploma in media communications or even, God help you, an uncle on the *Daily Telegraph*, but for my money a light touch, a long nose, and luck will get you further. I hero-worship two people. The first is the Irish writer Flann O'Brien whose wit, inventiveness and enthusiasm always make me laugh. The second is Alice who went down the rabbit-hole, eyes wide open, fully expecting a surprise on every shelf, in every bottle, round every corner. She was never disappointed and neither am I.

A week in the life of Sue Arnold

Another glittering week crammed with hectic engagements, all, it turned out, of a somewhat personal nature.

On Monday I went to the very gracious home of Marion, Lady Langham, in Belgravia, to inspect a revolutionary new space-saving, time-saving, money-saving personal hygiene appliance recently installed in her downstairs lavatory. Sadly, her Ladyship was not at home to demonstrate the novel all-in-one toilet-cum-bidet, but a genial young man called Brian did the honours in her absence.

I'm so sorry, have I given offence by mentioning such delicate matters? Come now, a bidet is a perfectly respectable (some might say indispensable) domestic item and if Marion, Lady Langham is good-hearted enough to allow the prototype to be plumbed into her downstairs lavatory, and public-spirited enough to have interested buyers and newshounds traipsing through her house to gaze in wonder upon it, then the least you can do is to read on. Where was I? Ah yes, the loo-det as I shall call it.

'Where is it?' I asked, looking about her Ladyship's gracious but somewhat compact cloakroom. There was nothing in sight but the standard loo and a sort of plastic lunchbox on legs with switches beside it. Brian clicked a switch.

'As soon as you come in, you press that to heat up the water,' he said. 'There, it's hot enough.'

He clicked another switch and quite suddenly a very strange and unnerving thing happened. From the dark recesses at the back of the lavatory bowl, a sinister silver spout with an uncomfortable-looking spray nozzle on the end of it, moved slowly forward into view. It was like something out of *Quatermass*. I watched in terrified fascination, totally unable to move or even cry out. Brian pressed another switch, whereupon a powerful jet of tepid water squirted out of the nozzle straight into my face.

'Damn,' said Brian, using his car keys as a screwdriver. 'Someone's been tampering with the nozzle. It should be at an angle of 45 degrees, no more.'

I tried not to think of Marion, Lady Langham tampering with the nozzle.

'It also dispenses liquid soap,' said Brian. 'Shall I show you? In fact, why not try the whole thing out for yourself?' he suggested, stepping discreetly outside on to her Ladyship's landing.

I remembered an urgent appointment in Wolverhampton and, with regret, had to decline; but I can see why the loo-det is such a winner – and, what's more, a snip at £350.

On Tuesday I was invited to Harrods to meet a very wonderful American called Adrien Arpel who had written a book called *How to Look 10 Years Younger*. It should have been called 'How to Look 30 Years Younger' because Miss Arpel, forty-one, dressed in a cute little flying-suit and sneakers, and topped with a baby-soft complexion, looked not a day over eleven.

'Honey,' said Miss Arpel, 'I'm going to give you my famous make-over shape-over treatment.' She could have added leg-over as well, for by the time I had finished hopping on and off beauty couches, cosmetic stools and hairdressing stools for four hours I was knackered but undoubtedly transformed. Miss Arpel's skin treatments include rubbing dollops of blood plasma, serum and plant algae into the face, but fortunately she then applied so many layers of wrinkle remover, eye-gel, sag-eraser and blot-out stuff that the contours of my face, let alone all the other yuk, were difficult to detect. Honestly, if like me you have a couple of hours to spare before breakfast to fix your face, you can't fault the treatment.

On Wednesday I attended a dazzling literary dinner in Manchester to promote my book – oh, didn't you know I'd just finished a brief but brilliant history of royal children? Hurry, write to me now for copies, I've got thousands. A director of Granada Television said, 'Ah, Mrs Armstrong, may I introduce you to the Lord Lieutenant of Lancashire,' and the Lord Lieutenant of Lancashire coughed and said, 'The High Sheriff of Cheshire, actually,' and David Frost told some jokes which made the Midland Hotel guests guffaw genteelly.

On Thursday I did my first aerobic dancing class. Of course, everyone with half an eye to health and fitness has been doing aerobic dancing à la Jane Fonda's bestseller for years but, to a congenital slouch and chocolate-eater like me, the prospect of such concentrated vigorous exercise is daunting. I took the precaution of asking Nancy Roberts to come with me. Nancy is that marvellous big, fat, jolly girl whose slogan is 'Big is Beautiful' and who is pioneering *haute couture* for over-eaters.

We met outside a fashionable Fulham health club where matchstick men and women with bronzed limbs, sweatbands and complacent expressions were wandering about. Nancy asked if they ran special classes for fat ladies. They said they didn't. Nancy said sadly that it was a shame, considering 47 per cent of women in this country are size 16 plus, and that she was going to start special health classes for fatties called Big, Beautiful *and* Fit.

'Go ahead, do your aerobic dancing,' she said. 'If I put all that strain on my heart I'd be dead in five minutes.'

I stripped down to my smalls and danced for an hour. It was called the beginners' class. God knows what the advanced lot do. Aerobic dancing is geared to cardiovascular exercise. With the tape recorder blaring disco music, twelve human skewers and I jogged and bounced and stretched and bent and crouched and leapt and heaved, and whenever there seemed to be a hiatus, our bionic Brazilian dance teacher ordered us to run at double-speed on the spot.

On Friday I didn't go to the launch of a new high-fibre restaurant or a party to introduce an individual-suspension sports brassière, or even to a demonstration of Zen gardening. On Friday I went to bed.

City Lights

Hurricane warning

At a quarter to two the waiter said I was wanted on the telephone. I stopped memorising the menu and followed him.

'Look,' said Alex Higgins at the other end (Hurricane to the snooker-playing fraternity but only Distant Thunder to ladies of the Press wanting to have lunch with him), 'I'm sorry I didn't make it. I'm waiting for my mother and my sister to come back from the shops. Why don't you come over and have a drink with us?'

'But what about the interview?' I said. On Tuesday Mr Higgins was favourite to win the Embassy World Snooker Championships.

'Sure, come and have a drink.'

There were ten people in the corner of the hotel bar and about thirty glasses on the tables between them. Mr Higgins, small, thin and habitually pasty-faced, put a pint of Guinness and what looked like a Pernod and Coke in front of me and introduced his father, his best man, his best man's wife, Eddy the former Irish amateur snooker champion, his friend Peter who's a jockey, his friend Peter's girl friend. . . They were all talking about Mr Higgins's recent appearance on 'This Is Your Life'. Eddy bought another round of drinks.

Mr Higgins revealed that he knew all along he was going to be on 'This Is Your Life' because his agent in Weybridge had been acting a bit odd and finally Mr Higgins had prised the information out of his wife Lynn. Still, not wishing to disappoint Eamonn Andrews, he had put on a pretty convincing show of total surprise and heartfelt emotion too deep for words.

The best man bought us all a drink and Mr Higgins's mother, sister and niece arrived hot from Oxford Street carrying seventeen carrier bags. 'I bought three pairs of shoes, two dresses and a jacket, but I'm not sure about the jacket,' said Mr Higgins's sister, who lives in Australia and was flown over by Thames Television for the programme. Mr Higgins's mother ordered a large gin, his sister a large vodka and, while he was about it, Mr Higgins bought everyone another drink. The jockey climbed over me and the best man's wife to go to the gents and I took advantage of the confusion to ask Mr Higgins whether snooker players were full of the same bonhomie off the baize as they appeared to be when on it.

At least I think that's what I asked, but Mr Higgins replied that the hotel was a real rip-off. He'd had to pay three quid that morning for two boiled eggs and the whites were all runny. Mr Higgins's niece, who was sixteen and built like Farah Fawcett Major, pulled down the hem of her purple-and-pink striped mini-dress to stop it throttling her and said she was going to freshen up in her room. Mr Higgins watched her leave in a loosely avuncular way and said he fancied a spot of Chinese. I eagerly offered to buy him several bowls of special fried rice if he would care to accompany me to the nearest Lotus Garden, but he didn't hear because he was too busy climbing over his father and the jockey's wife to go to the gents.

The barman returned and took another order from Mr Higgins's father, who was just leaving to catch the Belfast shuttle. Two drivers from Thames Television had now joined the party and the waiter was asking who had ordered Bacardi and tomato juice on the rocks.

Mr Higgins returned from the gents with Freddie Truman, a Dutch toilet soap executive and an unidentified man who quickly identified himself by buying us all a drink. Mr Truman and Mr Higgins had a lengthy and passionate conversation about prize money, promotion tours and how much you could get for television shows in Australia. They were both deeply appreciative of working conditions down under. The Australians, said Mr Truman, did not mess about. He was once offered a fee of 30,000 dollars and while he was recovering his breath the producer said, 'Well, maybe we could bump it up to 35,000 with expenses'.

The Dutch toilet soap executive bought us all a drink and gave everyone a bar of toilet soap with a picture of a thatched cottage and Good Morning written on the wrapper. Eddy, the former Irish amateur champion, said that when Alex was a little lad he used to mark their scores for threepence to get enough money to play at the little league tables. He also said that at the rate Hurricane was going he would probably flake out by the time he was forty-five. He was then thirty-one. Everyone who was vertical then bought drinks for everyone else.

It was now some time after six o'clock. I think Mr Higgins took me out to dinner to make up for missing lunch but, since by then I had long forgotten where I had put my notebook, the rest is silence.

Getting the needle

I was actually looking for an upholsterer when I came across Jock's Tattoo Studio opposite King's Cross and next to a sex shop.

I once read a ghoulish story about a prisoner who had had

his entire back tattooed with a still life by a fellow inmate who went on to become a world-famous artist. Years later the ex-con with the tattoo is shuffling along a Paris street, destitute, starving and ready to tip himself into the Seine when he passes an art gallery exhibiting, at astronomical prices, the paintings of his erstwhile buddy. Our man shuffles in, strips off his rags, shows the wheeler-art-dealer the tattoo, complete with artist's signature, on his back and asks 'How much?' I won't tell you the rest. I said it was ghoulish.

Anyway, an hour in Jock's Tattoo Studio seemed marginally more amusing than measuring loose covers, so in I went. A small toothless retainer led me through the foyer lined with pictures of tattooed torsos and designs – birds, beasts, saints, sinners and lots of naked ladies doing inventive things. Toothless Tich showed me into Jock's consulting room, where I beheld a curious sight.

Two young women built along the lines of Artemis and Hippolyta were wrestling over a Formica-top kitchen-table. The blonde was in a supplicating position, one leg bared to the thigh, thrust over the table top. The dark girl loomed above, pinning the other's leg in a variation of a half-nelson. The blonde was whimpering. On the other side of the table sat Vulcan, alias Jock, a giant of a man with pneumatic biceps, bushy black hair and a bushy black beard. With ferocious concentration and frequent bushy black expletives, he was tattooing a horse's head on the blonde's ankle.

'Try clenching your bum muscles a bit, Barbara,' said the dark girl, wiping blood and ink from the burgeoning tattoo with a piece of kitchen roll. 'It don't hurt so much then.' She spoke from experience. Her own limbs were beautifully illustrated.

I squeezed myself into a seat next to a sink and a suspended skull and watched the procedure with awe. Jock was a real craftsman. 'Why a horse's head, and what happens when you get sick of it?' I asked Barbara.

'I dunno,' said Barbara, lighting another Dunhill. 'I'm having a spitting black cat on me left shoulder next. I like cats.'

'How many layers of skin do you go through?' I asked Jock.

'Don't ask so many questions,' growled Jock. 'I'll go through fifty layers if you show me the money.' The money was bundled in an old cigar box in the table drawer.

The dark girl winked. 'Don't take any notice. He's a lovely fella.'

Jock is a second-generation tattoo artist. His own considerable skin area is covered with around 700 motifs, his name is engraved inside his lower lip and he has an amusing insignia round his neck which reads Cut Along The Dotted Line. His left forearm is a sort of sketch-pad for students; there's no original skin colour left. Business was fantastic in the 1950s, he said, with girls especially wanting Elvis and bleeding hearts *all over* them. It seemed pretty brisk now. While we talked Jock drew swallows, scrolls, flowers, panthers on the waiting customers.

A scrawny youth with DAVE imprinted on his shoulder wanted a devil with My Keeper written beneath. 'Sit down, Dave,' said Barbara.

'My name's Bill,' said the youth.

If the customers look too callow Jock demands to see their birth certificates. Legally you have to be eighteen to be tattooed. Jock got sick of irate mothers coming in saying Little Johnny can't get a job at the Pru on account of all those naked women up his arms. Jock can remove tattoos but it hurts, and what's more it costs. A trainee chef wanted a banner with his niece's name Karina writ large. 'Too late, sonny,' said Jock, who'd just written Carena.

Four enormous Swedes completely filled the room

demanding ping-wings, the emblem of their Rugby club, on their chests. 'If you mean penguins with yellow feet, strip off and sit down. It'll be £8 a penguin,' said Jock. The captain took his shirt off and sat down.

'Oooh, you've got a lovely young body,' said Barbara.

Had Jock ever been asked to do an impossible tattoo? I wondered. There was one design that looked more complicated than the roof of the Sistine Chapel.

'Never,' said Jock, wiping his electric needle with a Kleenex. 'I had a man in the other day who wanted his testicles tartan. Came up quite nice.'

'Good grief,' I said, momentarily stunned. 'Was he Scottish?'

'Never asked,' said Jock.

Hot stuff

Let us forget the fading fripperies of summer and turn our attention to the all-absorbing question of thermal underwear. The trouble with most thermal underwear, I am reliably informed by people in the business, is that it isn't all-absorbing, doesn't soak up body moisture – all right then, *sweat*, if we're being engagingly candid – and therefore doesn't work.

The secret ingredient of the real McCoy, the type that M. Cousteau wears on the sea bed, Mr Bonington up the Eiger and Clare Francis round The Horn, is something called thermolactyl, a cunning little fibre as absorbent as one-sided blotting-paper, as soft as syllabub and as tough as old boots. I can personally vouch for it. I am at present sitting here exuding heat like a freshly brewed pot of tea, thanks to an inner layer of lagging comprising one pale pink thermolactyl vest that comes to just above my knees and one pair matching thermolactyl knickers that come to just below my armpits. It is not, I own, a combination of garments designed to unleash uncontrollable urges in the average male, but it keeps me warm.

Actually, I'm not so sure that pale pink bloomers aren't considered sexy these days. Last winter, in what they now laughingly refer to as the 'cold snap', when Schloss Arnold withstood thirty-seven burst pipes, five cracked radiators and deep-frozen mice, I bought a pair of old-fashioned flannel drawers from a shop called Elsie's, in Haslemere's answer to the Avenue Foch. They were capacious enough to double as dust sheets for a catamaran, the colour of John West salmon, they had elastic at the knee, and I was so deeply ashamed of them that I double-locked the doors and drew the curtains before daring to put them on. I used to wash them out at midnight when the household was asleep and swaddled them in a sheet before hanging them on the line for fear the milkman would see them and make me a laughing-stock.

And then one freezing February day, standing on Rugby station waiting for a connection, the Glasgow Inter-City 125 thundered through, lifting my skirt above my knees and thus revealing to the world my terrible flannel underwear. I promise you that the fellow who hid his ass's ears under a hood could not have blushed more than I when my secret was out. As I stumbled blindly to the Ladies' Waiting Room to hide my shame, a pretty young girl came up to me and said, 'Excuse me, I couldn't help noticing your wonderful pink pants. Do tell me where you got them. My boyfriend is crazy about lisle stockings and flannel bloomers.' No wonder the Victorians had such large families.

Which leads me neatly on to another intoxicatingly

absorbing subject. You may have noticed that I have used no fewer than four words to describe the same item of clothing, namely knickers, bloomers, drawers and pants. There are many, many more. I have long maintained that just as those tedious lexicologists claim they can categorise you socially by whether you say parlour, sitting-room, drawing-room or lounge, I can immediately suss out a man's social standing and sexual proclivities by what he calls what I was always taught to call 'knickers'.

As a child at my convent boarding school we wore two pairs, white Aertex knicker-linings and a stouter outer version, commonly referred to as one's 'windbags'. These were made of hairy, heavy-duty navy-blue drill with a pocket on one side and a propensity to shine on the backside.

As a podgy teenager, I and my peers succumbed to the torture of a dispiriting garment called a panty girdle, a modern version of the Edwardian whalebone corset, designed to suppress superfluous steatopygous tissue. Aesthetically it was about as sexy as a boil-in-the-bag kipper and practically it was not much cop, because on the principle that what goes in must come out, where the elastic ended at diaphragm and thigh, huge wodges of displaced flesh accumulated like sandbags.

My grandfather's generation talked about 'drawers', and there were a number of genteel jokes on this theme.

'Winter draws on, Mrs James.'

'No, Vicar, but I've got two pairs in the making.'

Stand-up comics on the northern club circuit never fail to raise a laugh with 'bloomers'; chaps who escort girls who play squash and eat beetroot favour 'briefs'; middle-aged bachelors who wear slacks and do their own Hoovering prefer 'smalls' (as in, 'I won't be a minute, I'm just rinsing my smalls'); and ageing trendies, who still say 'groovy' and 'no way', smack their lips on 'ladies' knicks'. Lascivious bosses give their secretaries 'panties' for Christmas made of scarlet

Bri-Nylon with black lace bows. Washing-line snatchers go for 'undies'; male window-dressers called Adrian like 'lingerie'; and 'underwear' is a department in Marks and Spencers. But I digress.

I believe I was extolling the merits of thermolactyl as explained to me by a rather elegant gentleman called Jonathan who represents the largest thermal underwear company in the country. We drank white wine, and Jonathan told me that ladies' knickers made up 64 per cent of the total underwear market in Britain last year but only 4 per cent of these were thermal. It is, however, a bull market, and now that people like Zandra Rhodes are designing hot underpants, and manufacturers are going in for zappy colours, sales this year are expected to soar.

You may remember that endearing if slightly eccentric English priest whose vocation, he claimed, was to say mass on the ten highest mountains in the world. He was lost on some Peruvian peak for three weeks and when rescued said that only faith and his thermolactyl longjohns had saved him. It's a fairly formidable combination, after all.

The cold sell

'Congratulations, Mrs Arnold,' said a cheery male voice at the other end of the telephone. 'You've just won a year's supply of groceries from Farmhouse Foods.'

'Good heavens – are you *sure*?' I racked my brains. Had I bought any raffle tickets for the Conservative Party hoedown off my friend Marigold lately, or been first through the check-out with a pound of black pudding, or entered one of

those competitions where you have to write a poem about
floor polish in not more than twelve words? I remembered
penning a moving stanza about a new spray deodorant some
weeks back which ended 'O Twin-Pack Protector In Thee
Do I Trust' but I was sure that was for a weekend in the bulb
fields of Holland.

Perplexity turned to panic at the thought of a year's supply
of Rice Krispies being dumped at my door, followed swiftly
by a year's supply of large sliced white, Kit-e-Kat, soap
powder, self-raising flour and Jaffa Cakes. We would have
to convert the loft, build a garage, rent a warehouse,
move.

'How did I win these damn groceries?'

'Don't worry, we'll explain when we come round,'
chuckled the Farmhouse Foods fairy, who sounded as if
he'd just knocked back a year's supply of bromide. 'Why
don't we make a date? How about 7.30 next Wednesday
evening?'

All week we plotted what we would order. Of course
Gentleman's Relish and smoked salmon counted as
groceries, said my beloved, thumbing through the Fortnum's catalogue. I was hoping to swing a twelve-month
supply of low-tar king size and tights. We cleared out the toy
cupboard for the first delivery. At precisely 7.30 on Wednesday evening the doorbell rang. We heard footsteps climbing
slowly up the four flights to our flat, doubtless weighed down
by the first batch of plain chocolate digestives. I opened the
hall door and saw an elderly woman with wispy grey hair, a
bulging handbag and two inches of petticoat showing at the
back standing outside.

'Good evening, Mrs Arnold. I'm Alice Baker of Farmhouse Foods.'

In the kitchen Mrs Baker sat four-square at the table,
opened her bulging bag and took out a large black folder. She
placed it respectfully before her and clasped her hands over it

as if she were about to give a Bible reading. In a way she was. 'Was it the twin-pack deodorant or the Tory hoe-down?' I begged. 'Does brandy count as a grocery, *cooking* brandy naturally, how many people does it cover, is the baby included . . . ?' Mrs Baker raised her hand for silence.

'I am coming to that. Let us start with some facts. Tell me, how much do you spend every week on groceries?'

'I've no idea. It depends. If we have people for supper it goes up, if I've lost my family allowance book it goes down.'

'Give me an average week's budget,' commanded Mrs Baker, rapping the black folder impatiently.

'Well, I suppose around £40 –' (a sharp kick on my shin) – 'that is to say nearer £60 really, counting the milkman and the – er – dustbin liners . . .' I trailed off feebly.

'I am only concerned with food,' said Mrs Baker. She scrawled three columns of figures on a scrap of paper, added them up rapidly, divided by twelve and looked up in triumph.

'With Farmhouse Foods you could halve your weekly food costs, thereby saving yourself a year's supply of groceries,' she beamed and simultaneously as our jaws dropped she snapped open the black folder to reveal a picture of a deep-freeze the size of a hearse with the words 'Save the Farmhouse Way' written above it.

I suppose then and there we should have guided Mrs Baker to the door and booted her down the four flights of the stairs. The trouble was that Mrs Baker, warmed up and firing on all four cylinders, was almost impossible to switch off. Without pausing for breath she launched into a spiel whose fluency would have impressed the guide at Anne Hathaway's cottage. As she spoke, she turned the pages of the black folder, revealing more pictures of huge pink pork chops, bushels of glistening green peas and arctic wastes of vanilla ice cream, all to be had at rock bottom prices if we were to buy a ready-stocked Farmhouse Foods freezer for a mere £399.95 plus VAT.

In vain we said we rarely ate pork chops, hated frozen peas and were allergic to ice cream. In desperation we showed her round our cramped quarters. Surely she could see that there was nowhere to put an enormous deep freeze. Mrs Baker did not weaken. 'What is this wasted cupboard here?' she demanded, poking at a dark corner in the hall.

'That's our airing cupboard,' I said, stepping protectively in front of it lest she should demolish it on the spot.

'No need for an airing cupboard. Our upright model will tuck in there splendidly. You won't regret it. Just think of the saving.'

In the end we gave in. My husband poured three large glasses of brandy (*cooking* brandy), and we wrote Farmhouse Foods, care of Mrs Baker, a cheque for £39.95 as a deposit on our deep freeze which we cancelled in the morning. Call it cowardly, call it what you like. In a no-holds-barred contest for persistence I would back Mrs Baker against the Speaking Clock. Excuse me while I jot down a ballad in praise of fresh, free-range chicken using not more than fifteen words.

The carpet-baggers

Some time ago I had a special delivery from Kidderminster – to wit, half an acre of Wilton carpet which upon arrival significantly failed to fall off the back of the lorry or otherwise be shifted despite a deal of effort by the driver and by me. For several minutes we wrestled with the Leviathan roll of cream-coloured wool like a pair of prawn fishermen trying to land the Loch Ness monster, a spectacle which attracted no little interest from passing King's Road shoppers but absolutely no offers of help. 'Hang on,' I said at last. 'I'll see if I can get someone in the punk shop to give us a hand,' for to tell the truth offloading the thing was a detail – the carpet had yet to be hauled up five flights of stone steps to my flat.

I've always wanted an excuse to go into the punk shop. It's been there slap under my flat for close to seven years: sheer terror has prevented me from penetrating that sinister black interior into which youths with hair the colour of traffic lights disappeared and from which strange hoarse music throbbed.

A young man wearing what appeared to be nothing but a collection of cruel-looking zips held together with safety pins and bits of string was sitting behind the till next to which was lying a small human skull. There wasn't much merchandise on show, just a few pairs of heavily buckled leather trousers, one or two black rubber mini skirts with matching bras and a few very large T-shirts giving illustrated instructions for making your own Molotov cocktails. 'I wonder if you can possibly help me,' I said. 'I need someone strong to help me unload a carpet. Perhaps I'd better see the manager.'

'I *am* the manager,' said the human zip fastener in a friendly sort of way. 'Yeah, I'll give you a hand. I'll get Miles too. Hey, Miles,' he called and a second youth emerged from the shadows wearing a T-shirt on which Snow White was doing unusual things to the Seven Dwarfs and a pair of jeans with rubber treads on the knees like Pirelli tyres.

It took Miles and Mark half an hour to get the carpet upstairs. On every landing they stopped, removed an item of clothing, drank a jug of orange juice and answered the barrage of questions I plied them with to prevent them from deserting me in mid-flight. No, they weren't punks. Punks were things of the past or of the provinces. Go to a pop concert in, say, Cambridge and you'd see punks but not in the King's Road. Sure they'd *been* punks once. Mark's friend Joe had had the first Mohican hairdo in London, a dark green one-and-a-half footer that took three cans of hairspray to keep upright. Now Joe was just a dirty greasy biker, said Mark sorrowfully as one might talk of someone who'd narrowly failed to get a commission. 'He wears jeans soaked in grease and when they're wearing out he wears his new pair underneath to soak up the old grease. He's in removals,' he added.

What was the current fashion? Butch Nazi and fluorescent rubber. On Saturday they had sold out of rubber trousers at £70 a shot.

When I was a student I shared a room with a plump girl called Rosemary who, when she thought I was asleep, got out from under her pillow a pair of latex Bermuda shorts which she wore in order to lose weight. Something to do with sweat I think. I came across them by accident when I was tidying up and wondered nervously if she was some kind of fetishist. The label was reassuring. '*Jiffy-Knicks help you lose weight painlessly,*' it said, and anyway the colour, a sort of surgical pink, would have turned off the Marquis de Sade. At the end of term I came clean and told Rosemary I'd seen her Jiffy-Knicks and did they really work? She burst into tears and said she'd kill me if I told anyone about them.

Anyway, I said to Miles, tell me about the rubber craze. And don't rubber trousers make you awfully sticky?

Not if you cover yourself with talcum first, he said. There were a couple of very good rubber clubs off Oxford Street. At one, a brace of girls in rubber cat suits and two-foot ice cream cones stuck over their boobs came out on the dance floor carrying whips. They grabbed any stray bloke, chucked him on the ground and beat the hell out of him. It was a real laugh.

Maybe, I said, but possibly a bit of a shock for some unsuspecting chap who'd dropped in for a quick half before catching the 6.27 to Godalming.

'They'd never let in a straight,' said Mark. 'You've got to be wearing the right gear.'

The ascent was completed. I offered beer and victuals but they said they had to get back. Maybe if I could give the shop a little publicity . . . Certainly. The *only* place to buy bondage trousers, anarchy shirts and fluorescent rubber bras is BOY, next to the Methodist Chapel in the King's Road. Actually Mark said that business was pretty brisk, particularly the mail order. They export to Sweden, Japan, Australia, the US. 'Trash and Vaudeville', a large department store in Philadelphia, is their biggest customer.

'I'll take you to a rubber club if you like,' said Miles kindly. He looked at my woolly skirt and cardigan meaningfully. I daresay with the light behind me I'd pass muster in my wellies, my washing-up gloves and the baby's plastic pants.

'Thanks,' I said.

Gay night on the town

On Monday night I went to the Pink Hippo Ball at the Hippodrome in Leicester Square. The Hippodrome is a vast rococo building that once accommodated a curious meat-and-two-veg nightspot called The Talk of the Town, beloved of coach parties from Barnsley and famous for its extravagant floor show. I remember being taken there years ago as my first grown-up treat. I wore a purple satin evening dress with an overskirt of lime-green net and the top of the bill entertainer was, I think, Dickie Valentine. For his last number he got all the audience to join in the chorus, the words being written on a giant blackboard that came down from the roof behind him.

The Hippodrome is under new management now and they've turned it into a regular upmarket disco with expensive strobe lighting and live bands. Monday night is gay night and the Pink Hippo Ball was to raise money for an organisation called Gay Switchboard which offers a twenty-four hour telephone service for people with gay problems. This, I know, will further infuriate my friend in Islington who says his rates go to subsidise a gay Irish teenage telephone service (furthermore there was, he claims, a recent move to put on a late bus for the hookers of Argyle Square returning from work); but Switchboard is clearly a much-needed service.

Calls come from a variety of people – sophisticates wanting to know the names of gay clubs in Düsseldorf because they're going on a business trip, mixed-up and as yet unconfessed gays who want to come out of the closet but can't find the handle, hysterical mothers who've just discovered that little Kevin is gay and how can they put a stop to it *now*.

Switchboard gives addresses of support groups, counsellors, legal and medical organisations, advice when relevant, and sympathy.

When I arrived shortly after 10 o'clock, the main entrance of the Hippodrome seemed to be nothing but barricades and bouncers, as if the organisers were anticipating a stampede of gatecrashers. I checked in my coat. There was only one other person in the ladies' cloakroom, a pretty dark-haired girl in a man's dinner jacket and bow tie, like the Princess of Wales at a Birmingham pop concert recently. Many moons ago I went to something called the Alternative Miss World Contest at the London Hilton and the ladies' room was full of men dressed as women, hitching up their falsies and rubbing dark foundation cream over their six o'clock shadows. One man, called Steve, who had entered the competition as Miss

Moonlight, very kindly showed me how his falsies worked and took one out to demonstrate. It was about the size and texture of a tennis ball without the furry covering and, said Steve, you could put it through the washing machine on the 'delicates' cycle.

The Pink Hippo guests were a motley crew. There were perfectly ordinary-looking chaps in jeans and T-shirts and perfectly extraordinary-looking chaps in high heels, fishnet tights and plunge-front leotards. There were men in dark city suits with waistcoats carrying briefcases and men in running shorts and running shoes. The fashion seemed to be for leather bracelets with metal studs rather like some dog collars I've seen round the necks of the more ferocious breeds of bull mastiff. And the vast majority of the younger revellers had toothbrush moustaches. I fancied I recognised a few faces. Down the King's Road from where I live there's a pub that used to be famous because the Kray brothers drank there. It's now much more famous for being a gay pub and at closing time you can see scores of these slim young men with leather wrist-straps and toothbrush moustaches piling out on to the pavement – in a far more orderly way, I may add, than your average straight imbiber.

'Hello Sue,' said a voice further along the bar. I turned to see a gorgeous Britt Ekland lookalike in a strappy black cocktail dress and elbow-length gloves waving at me. 'What're you drinking? You came to talk to us a couple of years ago – Harrow Gay Unity, remember?'

'I remember going to Harrow,' I said, 'but I don't think . . .'

'Of course you don't recognise me,' he said. 'I expect I was wearing me Fair Isle jersey and corduroys, but this is a party, isn't it?'

Two girls came up and ordered lagers. 'How are you liking it?' I said. 'Great,' said one. Not bad, said the other, but not worth coming up from Leytonstone for. There was this place in Leytonstone that used to have a gay night on Tuesdays only; now it was gay Wednesdays, Thursdays and Fridays too, so why bother coming up the West End? 'Oh, the grass is greener and all that I suppose,' said her friend.

I missed the mystery celebrity and the cabaret because I had to get home to feed the baby, but in the morning I telephoned Gay Switchboard to find out how much money they'd raised. 'Over £8,000,' said Mike. 'And you missed Kenny Everett, George Melly, Dave Dale.'

'Come and have a drink and tell me about it,' I said, so Mike and his friend David came along – neither, incidentally, had a toothbrush moustache – and told me how hard it is to be gay in a straight society. At least ten per cent of the population (excluding Scotland) is homosexual and yet they can't get their own radio or TV programmes, they can't advertise in straight newspapers or on ITV, they can't kiss each other goodnight on the Tube.

I said the only time I'd written about gays was when I went to see an enchanting young cabaret singer called Mark Bunyan who described himself as the Noël Coward of Colliers Wood. I mentioned his funny shoes and received a sackload of vitriolic mail from people who started, 'All very well, for you to sneer, how would you like to be gay and live in Huddersfield . . .'

'I wouldn't much like to be straight and live in Huddersfield,' said Mike.

Going dental

On Tuesday I went to a lunch to launch a children's book called *My First Toothbrush*, which seemed mildly inappropriate since but half an hour earlier I had emerged from my own dentist's surgery with a mouthful of scrap iron, gums like sandbags and the depressing conviction that my current toothbrush would be my last.

'Do have some haddock and cauliflower,' said a jolly young woman in red, 'and I'll introduce you to our dental adviser who'll fill you in.' The dental adviser was called Graham. He had a practice in central London and three teenage children with only one filling between them. Graham said that when he qualified twenty years ago no one had heard of plaque and the desensitising injections were worse than the drilling. You don't have to tell me. I reckon the most shocking experience of my childhood, apart from playing sardines with Uncle Neville, was when the dentist strapped a rubber gas mask over my face and started pumping.

I'd better tell you about the book. It's the perfect gift for grannies to give their little treasures with their left hand, having already dispensed large bags of assorted sherbet lemons, barley sugars and acid drops with their right. The text, featuring characters such as Devilish Dan Decay, is mercifully brief and every bit as fatuous as, but far better illustrated than, the Mr Men books. This must make it a surefire winner with children who apparently crave Mr Men books more than they crave Opal Fruits. Drilled through the whole book to the back cover are two round windows through which you can glimpse one red toothbrush and one blue mouth mirror. There are also four magic disclosing tablets which you chew, rinse and spit out, thereby disclosing how much bacteria you have clinging to your teeth. It all sounds to me like an ace party game which granny will love to play. It could be called Plaque.

Graham told me two dental jokes (apparently there *are* only two) and then I was introduced to the inventor of the My First book series whose name was Alastair. It all started, said Alastair, with a book sponsored by Timex called *My First Watch*, same sort of story, same explanatory message, same window with a watch at the back. There is now a series of My First books published by Pan, including *My First Torch* and *My First Pen*. The beauty of the series, said Alastair, was its limitless scope, provided you could get the sponsors. Wisdom sponsored the toothbrush, Platignum the pen. Duracell the torch. But why not, I wondered, broaden the horizons? What about *My First Woodbine*, courtesy of W. D. & H. O. Wills, *My First Hangover*, sponsored by Alka-Seltzer, *My First Diamond* from De Beers and even *My First . . .* – well, perhaps not.

Alastair and Graham then had a serious discussion as to whether there were in fact *three* dental jokes and if so, who could remember the third; and I was introduced to the author of the book, a young man called Nick with a waxy pallor about his face indicative of too much time spent under artificial lighting writing books about toothbrushes. 'I am not a dental journalist; I am an author,' said Nick. He said he also invented health products like a delightful new herbal bath which you dropped into the water like teabags.

'Good heavens, I know those things,' I cried. 'Someone gave me some last week. They're revolting. Apart from looking so repulsive, like wodges of nose tissue floating about, one of them split and the bath looked as if it was full of pond life.'

Nick sighed. 'Did you say you were from the *Observer?*' he asked.

'Yes,' I said.

'I thought so!' he said sadly. 'I once wrote a play for the Hampstead Theatre called *Mad Dog*. It starred Marianne Faithful. Your drama critic Mr Cushman described it as "rock bottom".' He sighed again. 'It's a curious feeling to wake up on a Sunday morning and read in the newspaper that someone thinks your play is rock bottom. I don't suppose you like the toothbrush book either.'

'I certainly do,' I said. 'I haven't finished it yet but it starts very well. I shall certainly advise people to buy it.' You see, gentle readers, I am not all bad. What's more you have it here in cold print that I can be bought for as little as a plate of haddock and cauliflower and a red toothbrush.

I was next introduced to the promoter of the book who told me that cheese, being alkaline, was excellent for the teeth; and to the publisher of the book who said the electric water-jet toothbrushes were marvellous for flushing under bridgework. He had very large teeth. I asked Graham, the dental adviser, what in fact *was* the correct way to clean one's teeth – up and down, side to side, round and round or in one direction only? 'It really doesn't matter if you clean them with your left foot using a green twig while swinging from a chandelier,' said Graham. Everyone laughed. Was this the missing third dental joke? 'No, seriously, the most important thing,' said Graham, 'is how *long* you do it for. Most people brush their teeth for twenty-five seconds. Two and a half to three minutes is the perfect time. And you should brush your children's teeth for them until they're seven.'

Good. That's precisely the kind of clarification I need. I'll start brushing mine when they put on 'Sailing By' and when it finishes and that nice announcer starts reading the shipping forecast I shall stop. On second thoughts, an electric water jet might fit the music better.

'I'd like to adopt an elephant, please,' I said.

'Certainly, Madam,' said the lady at London Zoo, taking out a form with ADOPTION stamped in big red letters in the corner.

'I know you've got one called Polé-Polé because my daughter's class at school have already adopted him, but perhaps you could tell me a little about the others.'

Miss Chivers, from the Animal Adoption Scheme Office, ran her finger down a long list. 'We've only got one elephant at the moment,' she said, 'but it's broken up into £30 units. I expect your daughter's school – St James, wasn't it? – has bought one or two units, but there are still a lot on offer because an elephant costs £5,000 a year to feed and maintain.'

'That's funny,' I said, 'I could have sworn I saw two or even three elephants last time I came to the Zoo.'

'You're quite right,' said Miss Chivers. 'We did have two but one died.'

'What did it die of?'

'I'm not sure. They're doing an autopsy on it, I think.'

My father used to work for a timber company in Burma which used elephants to haul the teak. He told me a lot about tuskers coming 'on musth' and the complicated business of giving the animals their annual anthrax inoculation with a syringe the size of a bicycle pump and a gang of oozies or elephant men to hold it down. He also said that when an elephant died they burnt it in a huge fire that could be seen in

44

Prome, fifty miles along the Irrawaddy, but I preferred the legend about very, very old elephants quietly taking leave of the herd and shuffling off, trunks at half mast, to die in the elephants' graveyard. There isn't much space in Regent's Park for an elephants' graveyard unless you count the tennis courts or the helicopter pad at the American Ambassador's residence up the road.

'What did you do with the body?' I asked Miss Chivers.

'Body, whose body? Oh, the elephant. I've no idea. It isn't my department. In any case the public don't like hearing about that kind of thing. They're very sensitive. We had to stop feeding live rats to the pythons because the visitors got so upset. Now about the adoption scheme . . .'

Let me brief you quickly in case you hadn't heard about this marvellous new idea. Woolworth's and school dinners aren't the only victims of recession. The 5,000 inmates of London Zoo are also feeling the economic pinch. It isn't surprising when you consider the Zoo spends £100,000 a year on water bills alone (it's a very clean zoo) to say nothing of brooms, detergents, bedding and, above all, food. Did you realise that a sea lion costs £2,000 a year to feed and maintain, a tiger £1,500 and a gorilla £750?

Actually the sea lions and gorillas are OK because two rather senior executives from the Rank Organisation went round the Zoo recently and after serious deliberation with the trustees decided that Rank would sponsor the sea lions and gorillas. Don't ask me why. Maybe they thought that sea lions and gorillas had something in common with the company's corporate image. Sponsorship is a bit different from adoption. It's more expensive – between £500 and £5,000 a year – and the money goes towards conservation and education rather than herrings and bananas. Sponsors get their names on a plaque hanging on the animal's cage. Adopters get their names on a certificate alongside all the other £30 co-adopters, plus one free annual season ticket to the Zoo.

'Do you think it would be possible,' I asked Miss Chivers, 'to adopt a *whole* animal for £30 rather than two square inches of a lion? What about, say, a whole pudu or a whole blotched genet?'

'I think you'll find the deer and the cats come more expensive,' she said, consulting the list. 'I know a reindeer is £750 a year. Let's see, now, the rats and mice come cheaper. How about a chipmunk or a chinchilla?'

'We've got enough rats and mice at home,' I said.

'I think I could do you a fruit bat for £30,' said Miss Chivers, 'or possibly a stinkpot. They're both single units.'

'I don't think a fruit bat sounds very lovable,' I said.

'That's a reasonable opinion,' said Miss Chivers. 'I've never liked bats much myself. Still, you never know. Shall we go and see it?'

We walked through the Zoo. It was wonderfully sunny and a visitor taking a picture of a mother orangutan with her new baby had a newspaper patch over his nose and an ice cream cornet tucked into his breast pocket. We passed the ring-tailed lemurs with their extraordinary tails, striped like football supporters' scarves, held in the air like question marks. An alligator snoozing in the lush tropical undergrowth of his cage lacked only a cigar and a straw hat to transform him into your typical Miami Beach tourist.

We came to Moonlight World, home of the Zoo's nocturnal species. Miss Chivers and I peered uncertainly into cages full of rocks and logs and sand with occasional furtive scurryings in the background. 'Here we are,' she said. 'The fruit bat.'

Adjusting my eyes to the gloom I eventually made out a sort of clothes line with what appeared to be a dusty black umbrella hanging upside down on it. I looked at the fruit bat and for all I know the fruit bat looked back at me, but it was hard to tell. I had had visions of bringing the children with my free ticket to look at their adopted pet but somehow the fruit bat didn't fit the cheerful family group.

We adjourned to the reptile house in search of the stinkpot but we failed to locate it. Maybe it's now an extinct pot.

'I think I'll take a bit of Polé-Polé after all,' I told Miss Chivers. 'Has anyone got its tail?'

Life before birth

What a pity this latest report on the scandalous inadequacy of ante-natal care in this country didn't come out a bit sooner. I should have liked to discuss it with Mrs Baker, Mrs Bridges and Mrs Rankin, with whom I have just spent a considerable period of time in the ante-natal ward of a large hospital. It would have made a change from the usual meal-time topics, namely Mrs Baker's clots, Mrs Bridges' new kitchen, and Mrs Rankin's failure to find an efficient floor cleaner in any of the supermarket chains. Other patients came and went, but we four great-bellied matrons formed the hardcore of the ward. Since she'd been there longest – apparently within minutes of conception – in deference to rank we invariably discussed Mrs Baker's clots first.

'There've been clots in our family as long as anyone can remember,' said Mrs Baker. 'Me sister over at Crawley, me mum, me nan, we've all had 'em. Now I don't deny these doctors know their business but like me nan says, if clots is in the blood, they're in the blood.'

'Well, this is it,' agreed Mrs Rankin eating her jelly, little finger daintily cocked. 'It's the same with boils. And warts.'

I pushed aside my liver hotpot which had suddenly lost its savour and asked, since I had just arrived, where the telephone was. Mrs Baker jerked her head towards a door marked Day Room. As I left I heard Mrs Bridges saying, 'Just so long as he doesn't do it blue. I couldn't use blue in a kitchen.'

'It depends on the blue of course,' said Mrs Rankin.

'Well, this is it,' said Mrs Baker.

A very young, very pasty-faced girl was sitting by the telephone chain-smoking. 'I'm so sorry, are you using the phone?' I said.

She turned to look at me and said with an oddly triumphant air, 'You go ahead. I've done all the ringing around I need to. I've rung the Welfare, I've rung my solicitor and I've rung Terry.' She looked up at me expectantly.

'Er, why did you ring your solicitor?' I said.

'First I rang the Welfare to make sure they get me a flat soon as I come out of the home. Then I rang my solicitor about the court case. Then I rang Terry.'

'What court case?' I said.

'The Busted Bikers case. It was on the news on County Sounds radio. Me and Terry were sitting in this pub, see, with some of the other Nomad Hells Angels when we got busted by the Road Rats. I was knocked clean off my stool straight into the Space Invader. I could have had a miscarriage on the spot, my solicitor said so, but I'll tell you something. Once this court case is over no Road Rat and no Old Englander neither is gonna dare lay a finger on me. That's what Terry says an' all.' She lit another cigarette.

Whoever designed this particular maternity unit, one of Wren's contemporaries I gather, evidently believed that the Great Drama of Childbirth should be a public occasion. The labour ward was separated from the ante-natal ward by a thin partition through which we could hear every pant, groan and shriek. There is something unnerving about listening to

48

someone screaming loudly, rhythmically and relentlessly at
3 a.m., knowing that this is what you're going to be doing
shortly. And as if *hearing* the Great Drama of Childbirth
wasn't enough, we could actually see it for ourselves, too,
since we had to walk through the labour ward with our
sponge bags to get to the bathroom. One result of all this
publicity was that we became experts in obstetrics.

'They'll be putting her on an ECG shortly,' Mrs Rankin
would say nodding towards the screens.

'Wonder if she's done an MSU yet?' added Mrs Baker.

'Course if they induce her now she'll end up having a
section,' said Mrs Bridges authoritatively.

'I had to have my membrane ruptured last time,' said Mrs
Baker nostalgically. 'Nearly drowned the midwife.'

'No thanks, no creamed tapioca,' I said.

I once asked the midwife if they let the natural childbirth
exponents give birth in all those rather weird positions
they're always talking about, like in the bath or upside down.
Yes, she said; as explained in Sheila Kitzinger's *New Good
Birth Guide*, this was a hospital where you could do your own
thing. 'We had a woman in the other day who wanted to
squat on the floor,' she said. 'Well, that's all very well for *her*
but put yourself in *my* position. Where am I supposed to
be when the baby comes out – lying underneath like a
mechanic?'

I wish I knew who they choose to sit on committees and
come up with reports about the scandalous inadequacies of
ante-natal treatment in this country. Elderly men, by the
sound of it. They should have chosen me. I had an incredibly
pampered nine months. I put on masses of weight, I got free
dental treatment and I overcame a lifetime's aversion to
creamed tapioca. I was actually sad to leave Mrs Baker, Mrs
Bridges and Mrs Rankin when I finally graduated to the
maternity unit upstairs. Mrs Rankin said that maybe we'd all
meet up again here in a couple of years' time. Mrs Baker said

to count her out, she was stopping at two on account of her clots. She had to be sensible.

'Well then, this is it,' said Mrs Rankin.

The Mayor the merrier

I was invited on Thursday to a charity luncheon by the 300 Group, a newish and extremely vigorous organisation bent on getting more women into politics, and was enchanted to find myself seated next to someone called Mr John Bull.

'Good gracious, what a marvellous name,' I said. 'Are you in politics?'

'Yes,' said Mr Bull, a small man with heavy spectacles and a bustling air, and what's more Lord Mayor elect for Westminster with at least 600 official functions to preside over during the next twelve months, including several State visits at which he will read the welcoming address direct from the vellum.

'Not the *vellum*,' whispered a woman on the other side of me drawing in her breath.

'The actual vellum,' confirmed Councillor Bull loftily, buttering his bread roll, and the entire table fell silent, picturing the historic scene.

What is it about the Mayoralty that inspires such awe? I once spent an afternoon with the Lady Mayoress of Preston who had a pair of golden halberds mounted on either side of her front door, the blades cunningly wrapped in clingfilm to avoid discoloration. Aside from Mr Bull, the last time I had the privilege of meeting a Mayor was this last Christmas Day when I was lying flat on my back in a hospital bed. Forgive me for raking up what must seem like history to you, poised as you are for first cuckoos and mad March hares, but when you have spent as much time as I have of late staring at the Get Well Soon cards on the locker and wondering dispiritedly if it's sardine salad for lunch *again*, high days and holidays loom large in the memory. Ask M. Proust. Either that, or I am suffering from that form of senile dementia whereby I can't remember where I put the car keys but can quote verbatim every question on my A-level Latin paper.

Anyway, back to Christmas morning when I awoke to the sound of 'Silent Night' played by a brass band outside the window and the sight of two smiling ladies at the foot of my bed with scrubbed faces, backs like pokers and black be-ribboned bonnets. 'Merry Christmas, Mrs Arnold,' they cried. 'Please accept this festive token from the Sally Army,' whereupon they thrust a small package into my hand and moved on to Mrs Soper in the next bed. Tearing open the parcel I discovered a pink face flannel wrapped around a bar of pink soap, but there was scant time to dwell on my good fortune, for Sister was standing before me with a glass of sherry and a hot mince pie (it must have been all of 8.15 a.m. – at this rate we'd be into Boxing Day by lunch-time), saying could she straighten my covers because the Mayor would soon be here.

My good friend E. Mace, *Observer* travel editor, told me he once spent Christmas at Moorfields Hospital and thought he must have died, because when he opened his eyes a huge figure covered in spangles was leaning over him saying 'Peace, my son,' like the Angel Gabriel at the Heavenly Gates. It turned out to be the Pearly Queen on a goodwill visit. The Mayor who came to our hospital was female – a tiny, bright-eyed figure in a brown fur coat, like a hamster carrying an outsized handbag. She came into the ward flanked by a consultant, several registrars, housemen and

51

senior nursing officers, while the junior nurses formed a guard of honour at the foot of our beds. It was all oddly theatrical. If the Salvation Army band, who were now playing in the corridor, had suddenly struck up 'Kiss Me Kate' and the Mayor had whipped off her fur coat to reveal a sequinned sheath dress slashed to the thigh and then proceeded to cha-cha round the sluice with Mr Driscoll, the consultant, I wouldn't have been the least surprised.

But she didn't. She stood at the side of my bed, took my hand nervously as if she were frightened of catching something and said, 'This must be a very difficult time for you.' I wondered vaguely if I should kiss her ring or whisper 'God bless Your Worship!' but she had already moved on to Mrs Soper.

Actually Christmas in hospital was quite fun for the patients with the possible exception of Mrs Bracegirdle who underwent a three-hour emergency operation instead of joining us for Christmas lunch. Mrs Bracegirdle and Mrs Soper both had extremely high blood pressure which is why, despite frequent requests, they had been refused permission to spend Christmas Day at home. 'It's my body and I'm entitled to do what I choose with it,' Mrs Soper had declared the previous evening over her sardine salad. 'These doctors think they can talk down to you but I know my entitlements.' One result of Mrs Bracegirdle's operation was that Mrs Soper stopped talking about her entitlements. Instead she talked about the tiny spots of mucus they'd found in her specimen. 'How d'you spell mucussy?' she asked, looking up from the letter she was writing.

Days passed. Patients came and went, but I stayed on among my wilting flowers and rotting fruit. New Year's Day dawned and once again Sister stood before me, glass of sherry in hand, offering to straighten my bed, for the Mayor was on her way. What for this time? 'To give the first New Year baby £5,' she said.

I asked Mr Bull if kissing babies comprised any of his 600 official duties but he didn't hear. He was saying that as Lord Mayor he ranked second only to the Queen in the borough. He would follow her in processions. Kissing babies didn't seem quite his line, I thought. I can see why the 300 Group want more women in local politics.

Trouble on the brain

'I'm so sorry, I hear you haven't been well.'
  'Mmmm, that's right.'
  'Nothing serious, I hope.'
  'No. Well, yes, as a matter of fact, it was rather.'
  'Oh.' Pause. 'Er, what was, um, the matter with you?'
  'I had a brain tumour.'
  Silence. *'My God!'* Silence. *'Good grief!'* . . . etc, etc.
  I know it's a rotten trick to pull on someone who's merely asking a casual question, but when you've just had a whacking great hole cut in the top of your head and a lump *this big* removed it seems a waste to let them think you've been off with flu. That's what a locum GP said I had. I went to see him because it said on the aspirin bottle that if the symptoms persisted for more than three days you should consult a doctor and this was the fourth morning I'd had a headache. 'Did you have frightful headaches beforehand?' people asked me afterwards. To be honest, they weren't that frightful. I know migraine sufferers who roll about on the floor in agony as if they've been harpooned, and people who lie in darkened rooms with cucumbers over their eyes injecting themselves with painkillers like junkies. My headaches were undramatic

and could be assuaged with a couple of aspirins every now and then, but I'm a great follower of label instructions so off I went to this GP.

He was a dapper young chap in a country-squire suit and toothbrush moustache, who said there was a lot of flu about. He prodded my back, made me say 'Aaaah' and peered for a long time into my eyes.

'Just checking to see you haven't got a brain tumour, ha ha,' he said, straightening up. 'By the way, do you wear contact lenses?'

'Yes, sometimes.'

'I should get them repolished if I were you. Your corneas are a bit scratched.'

'Is that why I've got a headache?'

'No, you've got flu. Take two aspirins and go to bed.'

The worst thing about people who've had operations is their Ancient Mariner propensity to bore you to death talking about them. I'll be brief. Shortly after washing up the breakfast things next morning I had what I prefer to call a collapse but what everyone else called a fit, and was whizzed away in an ambulance. Five hours later I came to and after various tests and a brain scan was offered the information that I had a tumour the size of an egg on the top left-hand side of my brain, which had probably been growing for the last fifteen years. The only thing I knew about brain surgery was from *Suddenly Last Summer* and no matter how often that nice young Dr Moher assured me I'd be OK – the tumour was almost certainly benign – I *knew* I'd come out a cross between Frankenstein and a bashed neep. If I came out at all.

The other major problem, of course, was my hair. 'Will they shave it *all* off?' I asked.

'It all depends who does the op. Mr Richardson always takes the lot off. Mr O'Laoire just shaves what's necessary.'

Fortune smiled. That evening Mr O'Laoire came to measure me for the drop. Question time. 'If I have something the size of an egg in my head, what has happened to my brain?'

'Brains are very accommodating,' said Mr O'Laoire. 'They shift over to make room.'

'But what fills the gap when it's gone? I mean if . . .'

'Don't worry. You'll be OK.'

It was the bell that brought me round. I was lying in the Intensive Care Unit with plugs and wires and drips sticking out of me like an adaptor. I could see a row of other people with huge turbans round their heads like me. The bell kept ringing and someone shouted 'Fire alarm! Strap them in!' at which my nurse hastily folded my arms across my chest, tucked in my wires, tied wide webbing straps across me at intervals and holding the drip aloft like those pictures of The Lady with the Lamp trundled me to the door at a gallop. 'False alarm,' someone shouted. 'Take them back!'

The Atkinson Morley is one of those Victorian hospitals where you know that every penny is being spent on medicine not on frippery. There were twenty-two of us in the women's surgical ward with one bathroom between us and two loos. I do not complain. It's one of the finest neuro-surgical hospitals in the world; there were ladies there from Jordan and India who went straight back to the London Clinic after their ops.

On the fourth day they took off the turban and I could see the damage. A beautifully neat 8-inch V-shaped scar and an Elijah haircut, i.e. flowing at the back and bald in the front. 'Don't worry,' comforted my beloved at visiting time. 'You can rake it forward to cover the patch like Bobby Charlton. I'll buy you a nice woolly cap, it's winter after all.'

'I can't wear a woolly cap to Christmas parties,' I wailed.

'Mrs Arnold,' admonished a nurse with a mane of russet curls, 'you nearly lost your life and you're worrying about your hair. It's what's in your heart that counts, not what's on your head.'

'I know, nurse, I know. But what's in my heart is largely determined by what's on my head.'

Compared to most of the others I had it easy. There were patients in there with far worse problems: strokes, spinal injuries, un-get-attable tumours. One morning sitting in the bath wearing my new beret with gold flecks and feeling pretty chirpy, I heard the telephone ring. The staff nurse's office was the corridor outside the bathroom (I said there were no fripperies). 'Hawkins Ward. Yes, we do have a Mrs Arnold. No, I'm afraid I can't. I can only tell you that Mrs Arnold's condition is stable.' Ah, so *that's* what it means. And presumably if your condition is 'improving' you're half way up the motorway to Aintree.

So much for hospitals – if I were a man I'd marry a nurse, no question. And so much for some GPs – the dapper kind in check suits, at any rate. Four years ago another such GP told me I had flu and I had septicaemia.

One final word. The next person who tells me a joke about an Irish brain surgeon gets a punch in the nose. They're the greatest.

Colour me credulous

On Wednesday I found myself in a very dim reception room at the Waldorf Hotel listening to a stream-lined American lady called Carole Jackson talking about the importance of colour. Miss Jackson was wearing a cherry red suit with a royal blue ruff which perfectly complemented her cherry red lips and royal blue eyelids. She had asked two volunteers from the audience to come on stage and was busily pinning different coloured bibs round their necks to demonstrate which shade best suited their skin tone and personality type. The light had so disimproved by now that for all I could see Miss Jackson might have been demonstrating safety at sea. Someone suggested switching the slide-projector light on, which threw a weird sepulchral gleam over the proceedings and made the two volunteers look uncannily like the brides of Dracula. Miss Jackson, who has just written a bestseller called *Colour Me Beautiful*, seemed undaunted and prattled gaily on about pink pantsuits. In the end the first volunteer was sent away with strict instructions to wear nothing but varicose purple while the second, an apple-cheeked colleen of some eighteen summers, was advised to stick to shades of gasworks grey.

The nub of Miss Jackson's thesis is that every woman falls into a seasonal colour category. Once you know which season you are you choose clothes, make-up and accessories only in the thirty or so shades pertaining to that season, and as a result your life immediately assumes a new meaning, a new harmony. Honestly, until Miss Jackson realised she was not an Autumn person and therefore couldn't wear orange, she just *hated* looking at herself in the mirror. Now that she knows she's a Winter and wears only coral and magenta, people come up and say, 'Why Carole, you're looking *fantastic*. What is your secret?'

Miss Jackson is happy to pass on her secret. A personal colour consultation, which includes advice on wardrobe planning and personality, costs £30, and for £2,000 she will train you to be a colour analyst and set up your own practice.

A man in the audience raised his hand. 'What happens,' he wanted to know, 'if your wife is a Spring person and likes to wear black?' According to the Jackson plan only Winters can wear black. Miss Jackson opened her royal blue eyelids very very wide, pursed her cherry lips, and said, 'Well sir, I guess she can always wear black in the bedroom.'

Shortly afterwards Miss Jackson left for a nationwide tour to promote her book, so I missed finding out my own season, which left me in a fearful muddle. I suspected I was Spring but since no one had ever come up and said, 'Why Sue, you're looking fantastic, what is your secret?' maybe I'd got it wrong and I should in fact be wearing mahogany and trying to look like an autumn leaf. In a fever of anticipation I made an appointment for a consultation with Pam, a UK-based Colour Me Beautiful analyst. Pam was wearing black from head to toe and showed me into a room entirely devoid of colour – white walls, sofas, cushions. She rummaged in a suitcase and emerged with a piece of purple cloth which she tucked round my neck. 'Perfect,' she purred. 'See how it *lifts* your sallow skin tones. You are a Winter like me.' She then gave me a handy wallet with thirty-three tiny pieces of material inside and said from now on these were what I should wear. I liked the black and white and red but was a little uncertain about that very pale violet usually seen in hairnets.

We were momentarily interrupted by a tall blonde, also dressed entirely in black, who stuck her head round the door and inquired through a mouthful of cheese sandwich whether she should feed the dog. Pam explained that this was an interior designer friend from Holland. 'Is she Winter too?' I said.

'No, she's probably Summer but it's difficult to tell because she dyes her hair.'

Was I, she asked, a classic, a natural, a sporty, a romantic, a dramatic or a gamin type? As a guideline, she said that Princess Grace was a perfect example of a classic, Elizabeth Taylor a romantic, Liza Minnelli a dramatic, Farah Fawcett a natural . . . 'Hang on,' I said, 'Did you really say that Farah Fawcett was a natural? Last time I saw her she was having her picture taken on the roof of the Hilton in a Force 12 and not one hair, not one follicle on her head, was moving. If Farah

Fawcett is a natural, I'll lay odds Barbara Cartland calls herself a gamin.'

Pam said soothingly that looking natural took a great deal of effort. She said it was difficult to categorise me, a combination of several types was the best she could do. I know it's unreasonable – after all that expert advice and my pocket wallet full of coloured swatches – not to be feeling harmonious, but truth to tell I don't. I'd hoped for something a little more than Winter combinations.

Junior breadwinners

Quite by accident I got out of the lift on the wrong floor in one of those vast West End office blocks the other day, and instead of seeing a solicitor about a will I found myself in the midst of a group of mothers and children who, it turned out, were waiting to be fitted for a television commercial.

Now, kids in commercials have the same physiological effect on my teeth as squeaking chalk, but as every ad-man worth his expenses will tell you, kids can sell anything from lollipops to low-loaders.

So, you must understand, that as a mother of five I am sitting on a potential goldmine. Even the baby, sponged down and tidied up at the ends, could be sent out to earn a few bob. But how to crack this market seems to be something of a trade secret, so my chance meeting with the mums and kids was a heaven-sent opportunity to find out. I commandeered a stray child in whiter-than-white socks, slipped him a fruit gum and lined up with the rest of them.

The woman ahead of me, who had no fewer than three

breadwinners in tow, looked hard at my charge. 'Didn't I see Troy last Wednesday at the Shreddies audition?' she said. 'How did he make out?'

'Have you lost your tongue or something, Troy?' I said sharply. 'Answer the lady when she asks you a question.'

Clearly surprised at the sudden change in his benefactress, Troy replied sullenly that he'd missed out on Shreddies but thought he had landed two days' photographic work promoting swimwear for British Home Stores.

'That's nice,' said the woman, 'I'd go for photographic any day. That's where the real money is. Take Garth now – he's in *Oliver*, eight performances a week, matinees, bank holidays and what does he get? A lousy £6 a night. *Six quid*. It's not right, is it, Garth?' Garth, late of Fagin's kitchen, did not look up from his comic.

How had Garth come by his West End job?

'Through the agency. Young'uns, it's called. They're ever so good. They put on their own shows at Stratford.'

Good heavens. Stratford on Avon?

'No, Stratford East, near Leytonstone. Every Saturday morning he rehearses, don't you, Garth? He's got a lovely part in "Chim-Chiminee".'

'No, I haven't,' said our incipient Gielgud beneath his halo of flaxen curls. 'I'm in "Little Bit o' Luck". You always get it wrong, Mum.'

I bought Troy off with the rest of the fruit gums and he introduced me to some of the other children. The mothers had meanwhile gone into a huddle at the other end of the room. Occasionally, I caught snippets of conversation. 'You're kidding, Ida – £35 for a whole day's shooting. That's *criminal*. Saffron got £45 a day when she did that Winalot ad. Mind you, she had to put up with all them dogs. Nasty things, dogs, hair everywhere.'

I asked Ronette, a seductive eight-year-old with tresses like Rapunzel and black satin punk pants, whether she wanted to go on the stage when she grew up. Ronette sucked her forefinger thoughtfully, fluttered her eyelashes and giggled, just like she does in the bubblegum commercial.

I tried again. 'Do you spend all your wages on trendy clothes like your punk pants?'

'These aren't my best clothes. They're just for school,' said Ronette.

But when did Ronette have time for Higher Education in between her other commercial commitments? I wondered.

Ronette's mother, who looked uncannily like the one who has just discovered New Chicken Oxo, said the agency laid on special tutors if the children missed school. Ronette's older sister, Hayley, had got two CSEs and she'd had a really heavy schedule.

A blonde girl in dungarees came bustling out with a clipboard. 'Who's first for the fitting? Please follow when your name is called – Cleon, Dax, Jade, Cheryl, Dane . . .'

I followed the herd. No one seemed to notice. In a large bright room the art director, in jeans and sneakers, was standing behind a table piled with kids' togs. The children stripped off and stood docilely while two young women measured them. 'OK, Grant first. Height four foot seven, inside leg 20, outside leg 20. Can that be right?'

'Jade, luvvy. Slip into those fluffy buttonthroughs, will you – no, those are Cleon's underpants. I said the fluffy buttonthroughs.'

'Who is the hawk-eyed lady in velvet jodhpurs?' I whispered to the art director's assistant. The hawk-eyed lady was not apparently involved in the fluffy buttonthrough scene but sat slightly apart, chain-smoking.

'She's the art director's wife. She's here to make sure he doesn't mess about with us assistants.'

When was the commercial actually being shot?

'Heaven knows,' replied the art director's assistant, jamming Jade's backside into skintight shorts. 'We've got to kit out all these ghastly kids first, which could take forever.'

I left the fitting and wandered back to the gang of mothers. 'What's the gear like, Cleon?' his mother asked, wiping a smut from her offspring's nose.

'Lousy,' said Cleon. 'I wouldn't be seen dead in any of it. Anyway, dark green doesn't suit my skin tones.'

Blood groupies

It was a crisp, clean, clear October morning. A Salvation Army band was playing in the square, pigeons scratched around the fountain and two scarlet-coated Chelsea Pensioners were selling flags outside the station. It was the sort of morning on which young men pack in their insurance jobs and go off to join the Army, a morning for doing something different, something selfless, something *good*. There was a large grey van parked outside a modern office block with National Blood Transfusion Service written on the side. Of course. I would become a blood donor.

As I pushed through the swing doors humming 'Lili Marlene', I almost collided with a man who was coming out carrying a bucket and mop. Before I could change my mind, a young woman in a crisp white shirt came up to me and said, 'Hello, are you a regular donor? No? Well, thank you very much for coming, this way please,' and I was shown into a large room with a row of temporary beds covered with scarlet blankets at one end and a lot of rather pale-looking people drinking tea at the other.

Don't worry. I'm not going into gory details about the

injections and the tubes and the sight of my blood draining quite slowly into a sort of hot-water bottle that the nurse kept shaking gently up and down or the row of little test tubes filling up with scarlet, because I know some people are squeamish about these things. As I lay there feeling woozy but worthy, a charming Indian doctor with a goatee beard told me in a soothing bed-time-story voice all the things they might do with my generous contribution. They could process it in a number of useful ways, he said. They could separate the red cells, for instance, and wash them or freeze them or dry them like beans. They could siphon off the platelets and the plasma and extract a substance called Factor VIII which, if the fancy seized them, they might dehydrate and store as antihaemophilic globulin concentrate. 'If you're interested,' he added pleasantly, 'why not come down to the laboratories at Tooting and see all the products for yourself?'

'Excuse me, doctor, a woman has just fainted,' murmured a nurse. The doctor went off to administer, leaving me to the State-registered vampire who was still shaking the hot-water bottle like a set of maracas. And then I suddenly remembered (I suppose it was the equivalent of the drowning man having his life flash before him) that I *had* given my blood once before. It was years ago when I was a student hitch-hiking in Greece. We ran out of money in Thessaloniki and two Americans in the youth hostel told us we could get good money for our blood. They had done it several times. One of them had funded his entire European holiday by selling his body for spare-part surgery to a Midwest hospital. I think he'd got $500 for it which, he said, was a better financial proposition than selling off the parts separately. He had a serial number stamped on to his heel like a laundry mark, indicating that he was hospital property, and he spent a few minutes every day scrubbing at it hopefully with a pumice stone.

'There, that's it, I think,' said the nurse, unplugging me.

'Go and have a lie-down for fifteen minutes and then help yourself to tea.'

There was an almost party atmosphere around the tea-table. We ate biscuits and crisps, and an Irishman who worked for the North Thames Gas Board told us that in Ireland you got a silver pelican badge after twenty-five donations and a gold one after fifty – if you were still alive. The Irish blood bank, he added, operated on the time-honoured eye-for-an-eye principle – you gave them a pint of blood and they gave you a pint of Guinness. He stirred his tea moodily. An American girl in shorts who had been looking rather sullen said she had a very rare blood group and back home in Idaho she got $50 a throw for it.

'What group are you?' said the Irish gasman.

'WFN,' she said, which sounded more like a radio station. 'It's the initials of the first man who ever had it,' she explained, 'Wilbur Farrell Northrop.' She also said that she wouldn't have come if she'd known she was only going to get a cup of tea.

I said piously that we in Britain owed the success of our great National Health Service to a basic belief in charity – most hospital employees worked for practically nothing so we, the public, could hardly expect a handout.

She retorted that her English boyfriend regularly topped up his university grant by selling his sperm, and once a fortnight they both went off to a gastro-enterologist in Harley Street to participate in a lucrative sideline called gastric aspiration.

'What's gastric aspiration?' we all asked. Even the woman who had fainted perked up at the idea.

'Well,' said Miss WFN, 'we go into his surgery and they put tubes up our noses and into our stomachs and after a bit we throw up vital gastric enzymes for research. It doesn't hurt a bit once you get used to it. It only takes about twenty minutes, so it gives us time to read the *Guardian*.'

No one spoke for a long time. We drank our tea and ate our biscuits trying to envisage Miss WFN and her boyfriend reading the *Guardian* with tubes up their noses.

'What do they do with the vital gastric enzymes?' I said at last.

'I don't know. I think maybe they make vitamin B12 out of it,' she said. 'All I know for sure is that we get £7 every time. Of course, it does mean you can't eat a cooked breakfast.'

It had begun to rain. The band, pigeons and Chelsea Pensioners had gone. Tomorrow would be a better day to join the Army. But then they sometimes want blood, too, don't they?

Porridge days

For reasons too painful to explain at this moment, I found myself following a large notice saying Inmates' Visitors Reception, to which I duly reported one sunny afternoon recently to visit an acquaintance temporarily detained in Her Majesty's Prison, Pentonville. Five prison officers in pale blue shirt-sleeves and peaked caps were crowded into a small glass booth at the entrance.

'Who are you visiting?' one asked.

'F35791,' I said, fishing out the bus ticket on which the information had been recorded.

'Take a seat. You will be called,' he commanded sternly, like some senior celestial dignitary on Judgement Day.

There were dozens of visitors waiting in the rows of straight-backed metal chairs. Whole families were having impromptu picnics. I repaired immediately to the Ladies (institutions make me nervous) where a scrawny girl in sandals was trying to change a bald baby on the edge of a wash-basin.

'Can you lend us a mirror?' she said. 'You'd think the bleeders would give us a mirror to do ourselves up a bit.'

I gave her mine and held the bald baby while she frizzed up her hair. Her husband, she told me without emotion, was in for GBH. Again. Back in reception an officer was shouting 'Visitors for O'Reilly, Murphy, Singh, Al Akran, O'Shaunessey, Muraji, Salvatore . . . this way.' We were each given a form to fill in and directed to the main gate. Mrs O'Shaunessey rang the bell, and the rest of us waited like a school croc.

Keys turned, bolts slammed. A thin officer with gimlet eyes inched open the door and seemed reluctant to let us in. Another waiting room, more like a corridor, with a small, Formica-top table and benches round the walls. 'Fill in your forms and wait to be called upstairs,' was the next order. A fat, kindly woman with one leg lent me a ball-point.

'Have you brought him anything? 'Cos if you have, you'd best check it in quick,' she said, skilfully manoeuvring her crutches along the corridor. 'They start timing your visit the moment they call your name. I took six minutes to get upstairs, and they stopped it off my time.'

I trotted after her, gleaning more information. We passed a notice listing prison regulations. Rule 5 said, 'Fees or gratuities to prison officers are strictly prohibited'.

'If you've got any food, it's got to be in plastic containers. No metal allowed. All books must be paperback,' continued my new friend.

Why not hardbacks?

'In case you hide secret messages inside the covers.'

Everyone had brought stacks of food, prawn curries, shepherd's pie, rice puddings. The one-legged woman had three Tupperware bowls of steak and kidney pudding. 'He loves his steak and kidney,' she said fondly. 'Funny, really, seeing as he's Egyptian.' An officer behind the hatch itemised everything. 'Bananas, Fyffes, seven, one damaged.'

'I've brought him some clean underpants and vests,' said a woman with tangerine lipstick and turquoise eyelids. 'Can I collect his dirties?'

'I'll get them sent over,' said the officer, packing the Y-fronts in with the bananas.

I produced my offering: four paperbacks, three packs of chewing gum and ten panatellas.

''ere, 'old on, nothing for F35791,' said the officer, pushing my parcel back at me. 'He's a CP, isn't he?'

A CP? He made it sound like BO or VD. I sensed a frisson of hostility in the cottage-pie queuers waiting behind me.

'CP. Convicted prisoner, that's wot he is,' said the officer smugly. 'No presents. CPs have the privilege of working, see? They can buy their necessary requisites.'

Not even the books, I pleaded?

'All books have to be sent into the library department for official inspection,' he said. Of course, silly of me. Someone had to check for microdot messages.

More waiting. I'd been there an hour and a half for a fifteen minute visit. A voice from above started shouting again. More names. We hurried upstairs.

Considering his unexpected incarceration, F35791 was looking pretty perky. He said he'd just got his week's wages, 75p; well, 73p after stoppages.

'Are you sewing mailbags?' I asked.

'No, cleaning the chapel,' he said, gloomily. 'We've got some Roman Catholic cardinal coming to consecrate it, so the screws are really on our backs. Leave your dog-ends as long as possible, by the way. The boys who clean up afterwards share them out.'

'Are you allowed to smoke?' I opened the box of panatellas.

A prowling warder loomed down on us. 'No unauthorized presents for prisoners,' he snarled, seizing the box.

'But everyone else is smoking.' I said.

'Oh, I thought it was a bar of chocolate. Carry on.'

F35791 said he was sharing a cell with a chap who swallowed 50p pieces as a hobby and nicked cars and credit cards as a profession. When the police picked him up he had forty-seven sets of car keys on him. F35791 said if he stood on his bed he could just see the corner of the pub opposite in the Caledonian Road, which depressed him a bit.

'Come on, Table 10. Your time's up. Finish off that cigarette,' snapped our friendly warder. 'Any longer, and he'll forfeit his next visit.'

I read in *The Times* the other day that they've just closed down the Pentonville Visitors' Centre run by volunteers because of the prison officers' unhelpful attitude. Surprise, surprise.

How the spirit was willing in Lewisham

At six o'clock on Thursday evening in a chill cheerless drizzle, the MV *Enchanter* headed east from Charing Cross Pier to Greenwich for an evening's paranormal entertainment. Our hostess was Mrs Doris Stokes, world-famous medium, now about to launch her third book, *Innocent Voices In My Ear*. I sipped white wine and chatted to Mrs Stokes's theatrical promoter, who said she had filled the Sydney Opera House three nights running, but in Baltimore she had run into stiff competition in the form of a psychic dentist called Ebenezer Hardbent, whose talent lay in inviting members of the audience on stage, looking deep into their mouths and turning all their fillings into gold. Yes sir – real, 22-carat gold. No kidding.

Doris was sitting on a dais like a Viking queen, in an apple-green frock, all soft white hair and pink cheeks, and smelling faintly of apple blossom. She took my hand and patted it warmly.

'Tell me,' said the world-famous medium and clairvoyant, 'haven't I seen you somewhere before?'

'What exactly are you going to *do* this evening, Mrs Stokes?' I said.

'Better ask that fellow, he's secretary of the SAGB,' said Queen Doris and passed me on to Tom Johanson of the Spiritualist Association of Great Britain, a grey-haired man with a lined face who said he was a psychic healer. His wife, Coral, is a psychic portrait-painter and merely by grasping your hand and looking deep into your face can come up with an uncanny facsimile of your late granny. Mr Johanson said he first became interested in spiritualism when an old friend called Johnny introduced him to a medium who could materialise spirits from 'the other side'. The medium had proceeded to materialise a middle-aged man in a grey suit, starting from his feet.

'Good heavens, it's Walter,' said Johnny. 'I was talking to you only last week. You're a fake.'

'No, I'm not,' said Walter. 'I'm dead. I was killed in a car crash two days ago. You ring my wife and ask her.'

'And had he?' I asked Mr Johanson.

'Yes, he had. His wife said it was quite true.'

I should have liked to pursue the matter further but unfortunately the roof of the Greenwich Observatory hove into view and we all disembarked into coaches for the short drive to Lewisham Concert Hall.

There were big notices on the door saying 'Sold Out' and a great many elderly women in pink cardigans and spectacles with pearlised frames were streaming into the auditorium. The stage was bare save for a table, two chairs and a rubber plant. There was an air of restrained excitement.

'I believe she's ever so good,' said my neighbour to her friend. 'Edie saw her in Wythenshawe last year. She brought Arthur back you know, clear as day.'

'Really? Well, I never. Is that one of those Indian skirts you roll up in a stocking to dry, that woman's wearing?'

'Ladies and gentlemen, may I present Mrs Doris Stokes,' said a thin young man who edits *Psychic News*, and Mrs Stokes settled herself opposite him with the air of someone about to have a nice natter. Which is really all she did for the next two and a half hours, except it was a three-way natter because she was also talking to a crowd of people on 'the other side'. This is roughly how it worked.

'Now don't be shy, ladies and gentlemen. There's nothing terrible going to happen. One of my voices will lead me to a contact and we'll take it from there. All you need is love. What's that you're saying . . . ?' (Here Mrs Stokes lifted her head as if addressing someone hanging from the ceiling.)

'Wilson? Watson? Yes, all right, love, Watson – let's see, where is my light going, ah yes, ten rows back in the stalls, lady in a pink cardigan, d'you know the name Watson, love?'

'My name's Watson.'

'Right, love, I've got someone on the other side who wants to say something. Does the name Nellie or Norah mean anything?'

'My mum's name was Nellie.'

'I've got your mother spirit-side, love, she says you'll find the £94 in the wardrobe in your bedroom – top shelf. Have you got a wardrobe in your bedroom, love?'

'Yes I have, but I don't know . . '

'Never mind, love. Your mother's telling me something about a new cooker. Do you know anything about a cooker, love?'

'Blimey, I'm getting a new cooker this week.'

'Well, your mother says you're to get the best you can afford because you deserve it. Now wait a minute . . .' (Mrs Stokes shook an admonishing finger at the ceiling.) 'Don't all talk at once. Who have we got? Peter? Three rows back on the left, anyone know a Peter on the other side? Yes *you*, love, have you got someone called Peter spirit-side?'

'No.'

'Sorry, love, wrong contact. Wait a minute. It isn't Peter, it's Potter. What about Potter, love?'

'My aunt was a Mrs Potter, she passed on last November.'

'I've got your aunt here, love, she's saying something about April. Hang on, she's singing "Happy Birthday". Is there anyone in your family with a birthday in April?'

'Yes, my sister-in-law's boy Neil had a birthday in April.'

'That's it, love, she says give Neil her love, and don't worry about her . . .'

In the ninety minutes before the interval, Mrs Stokes pinpointed the widow of a man who had died poking the fire, the daughter of a Scottish shopkeeper who had had a heart attack, and the owner of a black cat called Smokey living at number 12 Crawley Road. As I tried to fight my way to the exit past the queues waiting to buy her book, I wished irritably that I'd asked Mrs Stokes the way to the nearest mini-cab office.

Caught in the act in Flood Street

Do me a favour, someone, and buy Mrs Thatcher's house. It's not a bad old pad as £250,000 neo-Tudors go. I know because I was in it once, briefly I admit – just long enough for Mrs Thatcher, resplendent in peacock morning robe (it was breakfast time), to ask me to leave *immediately*. But the hall was nice and what I saw of the dining-room looked cosy enough.

I have nothing personal against the lady. Indeed, when she was but a lowly Secretary of State I once stood shoulder to shoulder with her in the Flood Street vegetable stall queue and discussed the shocking price of purple sprouting broccoli. It is simply that I have the misfortune to live almost opposite her – not, I hasten to say, in a mock-Tudor number, but in crumbling rented premises above a motorcycle repair outfit. We may not share a lifestyle but we share an address and also (here's the nub) the pitifully small number of parking bays offered to Flood Street residents.

Now, of the scant two dozen or so residents' parking bays up our end of the street, Mrs Thatcher has sole and exclusive use of eleven. Honestly, eleven. No, she doesn't have eleven cars. As far as I know she doesn't have any cars at all. The eleven bays are occupied by a series of bright yellow bollards bearing the message POLICE NOTICE NO PARKING. In the last five years I should say (this of course is a conservative guess) that Mrs Thatcher has visited her house at number 19 Flood Street maybe three times.

At about noon one filthy February day this year I returned

from a weekend away with a car full of five children, a Siamese cat, a rocking horse and a plethora of luggage. It was raining Persians and Shih Tzus (this is Chelsea, after all) and, there being no vacant resident bay for half a mile, I elected to park on the single yellow line outside my front door. As luck would have it a traffic warden was directly in front of me booking the driver of a yellow VW.

'Ah, Mr Traffic Warden,' I cried. 'Could you please bear with me while I escort five children, a Siamese cat, a rocking horse and a plethora of luggage up five flights of stone stairs without a lift?' The traffic warden waved his hand in peremptory fashion and I began a series of laborious ascents. Six minutes later, when I descended for the eighth time to collect the baby and the horse, I saw that I had a parking ticket.

I wrote to the Fixed Penalty Office stating what I thought to be pretty mitigating circumstances. Time passed. The cherry trees outside number 19 blossomed. I had a letter from the Chief Clerk at the Fixed Penalty Office declaring that my reasons were not mitigating enough, and unless I paid the fine I would be taken to court.

I wrote to the Chief Clerk saying that I would be delighted to go to court and state my case. Time passed. The cherry trees outside number 19 shed their blossom. I had a letter from the Chief Clerk of the Fixed Penalty Office reminding me that if I did not pay the fine immediately I would be taken to court. I reiterated that I would prefer to go to court. Time passed. The roses outside number 19 blossomed. I went to Burma, to Singapore, to Ballymaloe. I had a letter and a sheaf of forms from the Fixed Penalty Office asking me all manner of questions about the alleged offence.

I dashed a note to the Chief Clerk at the Fixed Penalty Office saying that I was just off to the Hebrides, that I admitted to being the driver of the vehicle on the said date in February and please, please, please could I go to court? On my return I found a letter awaiting me from a Mr A. Austin on behalf of the Officer in Charge, pointing out that my failure to fill in the forms 'as legally required' meant that I would no longer be charged with the original parking offence but instead for 'failing to comply with a notice to owner of vehicle contrary to section 1 (6) of the Road Traffic Act 1974'.

I gave up. The fire has quite gone out of me. I had had visions of myself in a picture hat standing in the witness box telling a hushed courtroom the tale of the five flights of stone stairs, the five children, the Siamese cat, the rocking horse and the luggage. 'I beg you, Mrs Arnold, please distress your-self no further,' the judge would say, struggling to keep the emotion out of his voice . . .

Alas, this is not to be. I shall pay the fine. There is no romance in failure to comply with section 1 (6) of the Road Traffic Act.

Do me a favour, someone, and buy Mrs Thatcher's house.

Creature comforts

'Just a goldfish,' I said. 'And a bowl, of course.'

'No bowls,' said the young man. 'We do fish tanks from £5.75 to £300.'

'Why no bowls?' I said. Even the £5.75 tank looked as if it could accommodate a barracuda in comfort.

'We had a fish expert along who said goldfish got very bored just swimming round and round all day long,' said the young man. 'With a tank you can introduce a variety of eye-catching features in every corner – a coral arrangement perhaps, or some interesting shells.'

'How much would the cheapest goldfish and tank cost?' I asked. 'It's only a birthday present for a seven-year old.'

The young man smiled politely. 'Well, let's see now. You could get a reasonable goldfish for £1.50, then the tank, £5.75, then you'd need a couple of scoops of gravel for the bottom, £1, two coral branches say £2, a selection of shells, a water purifier and some fish food and conditioner. Shall we say £12 the lot?'

'Tell me honestly,' I said. 'Do you think a goldfish is worth £12? I know it was aeons ago, but I can remember winning a goldfish at a fair for sixpence, and it lasted three years.'

The young man thought about it. 'For a seven-year old? Frankly, no.' He ruminated further. 'He'd get a kick out of the novelty for a week or so, but remember the fish have to be cleaned out every other day, and for a child that can be a drag. Besides, goldfish are basically uninteresting creatures.

We were standing alongside one of the £300 tanks. It appeared to have a battery of disco strobes and half of Kew Gardens inside. About thirty tiny iridescent fish, some striped, some spiked, some with fenestrated tails, were zapping about.

'What about that sort of thing?' I said.

'They're tropical fish. Beautiful, but troublesome,' said the young man. 'The water has to be kept at a constant temperature, the light has to be regulated and you have to know which breed gets on with which, because some tropical fish eat others. Those, for example, eat those.'

'What are those?' I said, pointing to the cannibals.

'They're £2.25 each,' he said. 'Golden somethings. Anyway, the £2.25 ones eat the 80p ones.'

It seemed fair.

'Just say I steer clear of fish altogether,' I said. 'How about a bird?'

'You could have a budgie,' said the young man without

enthusiasm, 'but with a budgie you need accessories – a cage, of course, and a few toys, a two-way mirror, a cantilevered swing, and here's what we're selling most of these days, a budgerigar shower. I'll show you.'

We moved to the budgie corner where a bedraggled blue and yellow bird was standing, stock-still, in a plastic shower cubicle while a jet of water from a yellow spray wooshed fiercely over its head and feathers. We watched for a minute in silence. The budgie did not move. 'I think he's been drowned,' I said.

The young man banged on the cubicle with his hand and said, 'Tweet, tweet'. The budgie did not stir. 'He's probably fallen asleep,' said the young man, trying to keep the anxiety out of his voice. 'Elaine,' he called. 'Can you come and look at Billy Jo, please.'

He guided me from the bird corner. 'Have you ever thought seriously about a hamster?' he said. 'Not a gerbil, they can be temperamental. But a hamster is perfect for a small child. Easy to care for, trouble-free, low running costs, high on amusement.'

We reached the central display area, where a lot of round transparent plastic tubes were stacked on top of each other. 'What are they?' I said.

'Hamster hutches,' said the young man. 'Unfortunately, you can't see any hamsters because they are all asleep in the tubes.'

'You mean hamsters *live* in those plastic tubes?' I said. 'I thought they lived in wooden cages.'

'Not any more they don't. We had a hamster expert in who said they thrive better in mobile situations.'

'How much do these villages cost?'

'A basic unit is £10, and then you can add any extras you like. An attic bedroom maybe, or a playroom like this.' He pointed to a small cake tin almost entirely filled with an upright wooden wheel. Hamsters, according to the hamster therapist, like nothing better than going round and round on a wooden wheel. Goldfish would just get bored.

'If they're nocturnal,' I said, 'do you have to flush them out of the tubes when we buy them?'

'No, you can see our Asian hamsters any time,' said the young man. 'They live in ordinary cages. They are £3.50 each, but they do better in pairs.'

'Give me a minute or two to think about it,' I said.

It wasn't easy. A jaded goldfish, a comatose budgie or a tube-dwelling hamster. In the end I bought a book about killer whales. Next year I'll get him the real thing.

Doorkey talkie

The one thing that needles me about not being married to a millionaire, apart from the money, is that I have nothing worth stealing and therefore no excuse to install one of the amazing new talking burglar alarms I heard about the other day.

Of course you don't have to be rich to be burgled. Thieves are not always accurate with their market research. We have been raided twice, the second time precisely eight days after the first, so that we hadn't got round to replacing the gramophone, the camera, the milk money or the front door lock, which left the second lot a pretty poor bag – two bottles of gin and a silver-plated dressing-table set which had sensibly been spurned by the first comers. The detective who came round to sprinkle fingerprint powder over the furniture said glumly that, living in Chelsea, we could expect to be burgled once every two years. He added that if the rotters really wanted to get in no amount of closed circuit television or Fort Knox hardware would deter them.

I have a very well-heeled (and incidentally very miserable) friend whose mansion is so wired up with security systems that if you stand too close to the glass case full of Ming trinkets an alarm goes off and the local SAS leap in firing from the hip. Every door and windows is cased in an iron concertina grille, and his locking devices are so sophisticated that on a couple of occasions he has been unable to get *out*. Needless to say, he was done the other day, in broad daylight. The burglars lobbed a brick through the bullet-proof glass of the dining-room (the grille was being repaired) and climbed in. The brick landed on the highly polished surface of the Hepplewhite dining-table, scoring a deep rut down the middle. There's a moral there somewhere.

But back to the talking burglar alarm. This is how it works. Every one of your domestic apertures is wired up to a central computer which, along with the usual silicon chips and stuff, is fitted with a voice. Every five minutes the computer does a round of the house sounding, I suppose, something like this.

Computer: Back door, calling back door. How're you doing, me old son? Anything to report?

Back door: Not a dicky bird. Haven't seen a soul all morning apart from the milkman and a couple of Jehovah's Witnesses. Isn't it today Her Ladyship's driving instructor comes?

Computer: He's already gone upstairs. Came in by the side entrance. OK then. TTFN. French windows, calling French windows. How's it going, my little mullioned beauties? Anyone been tampering with your catches or fingering your knockers lately?

French windows: Chance would be a fine thing. Honestly darling, a girl could die of boredom out here.

Computer: Hang on a sec, luvvy, I think I can hear

something. Is that you, Guest-room Dormer? Are you receiving me?

Guest-room Dormer: Mayday Mayday. I thought you'd never answer. There's a fellow with a stocking over his face and a sack on his back marked 'Swag' trying to shove a jemmy up my . . .

Computer: Take it easy, sweetheart. I've got it taped. The whole house is on red alert, the guard dogs are being unmuzzled and PC Bigginshaw is looking for his bicycle clips. Don't try and tackle him on your own . . .

You see why I want one. Never a dull moment. Apparently this talking lark is really taking off. I went to a do the other day to launch a new sort of electronic voice which you can fit into anything, your cooker, your car, your filing system. The miracle of the thing, said the man from Digitalker, the company that markets the voice, is that it isn't a robotic voice, it's a human voice. You could get Mrs Thatcher telling you the schnitzels were ready or Enoch Powell plugged into your car battery reminding you he needs topping up. Don't ask me how it works – the Press handout was a bit thicker than the Old Testament and the man I spoke to admitted that Digitalker voices were best suited to highly complicated electronic systems like the dashboard of Concorde or the Post Office accounts computer. He very obligingly showed me a simple example.

'See this coffee machine,' he said. 'I'll switch it on and you can hear what it says.'

He switched it on. The coffee started to bubble. A light flashed, a buzzer buzzed. 'Good morning,' said the coffee maker. 'Your tea is ready.'

A little run down

Strolling down Duke Street, St James's, the other morning on my way to Fortnums to have coffee with a lady who wrestles in mud, I narrowly escaped death at the hands, or rather the wheels, of one of those laundry vans that race around London changing soiled roller-towels and refilling soap dispensers for large corporations. I was not jay-walking, neither was I fantasising, oblivious of my surroundings, about what it must be like to wrestle in mud. The van simply mounted the pavement, scattered pedestrians and screeched to a halt next to a shop window.

Unpinning myself from some railings, I pointed out to the driver that pavements were for pedestrians. With slow, measured movements like the rumbling of a grandfather clock about to strike, he got out of the cab (he was a large bushy fellow with one gold earring and the sort of physique that swallows roller-towels whole) and suggested, in a manner of speaking, that I take myself off. Lacking a sling and a pebble, I concurred, plotting vengeance. I told the lady wrestler, who was also large and bushy with one gold earring, of the encounter, and when we had finished our coffee and mixed cream fancies we returned to Duke Street to set the record straight. Alas, the bird had flown.

So much the sweeter was it then to receive, a few days later, a letter from the Hon Sec of the Pedestrian Association, a Mr Cyril Myerscough, who drew my attention to the association's current campaign against pavement abuse by motorists – the driving over, the parking on and the obstruct-

ing thereof. Mr Myerscough pointed out that it was the
Pedestrian Association which had pioneered such breakthroughs as the Belisha beacon and the 30 mph speed limit
but, whereas they were a force to reckon with back in the
1930s, their numbers had now dwindled to around a
thousand souls – or pairs of soles.

This does not surprise me. While it is logical to suppose
that inside every motor car there lurks a pedestrian waiting to
get out, this is actually not the case. I know a number of
people who never walk anywhere at all, apart from the few
paces from doorstep to driving seat. One in particular, a
high-powered lawyer, complained to me recently that he was
putting on weight. I quizzed him about his daily routine and
it transpired that he went from his bed to his car to his office
to the lift to his desk to the director's dining-room, back to
his desk to the pub across the road to his car to his flat to his
bed. If that makes him a pedestrian, then I'm a six-foot
blonde trombonist.

The vexed question of pavement abuse is further complicated by the fact that the simple adage 'Four Wheels Bad,
Two Legs Good' does not always apply, for it is not the
good-hearted pedestrian alone who uses the pavement. We
must share it with a host of aggressive free-wheelers like the
pushchair militia, the skateboard fanatics, the roller-skating
nuts and, worst of all, those mild grey-haired little old ladies
with wicker shopping-trolleys.

I forgot to mention that my paunchy lawyer thought he'd
shift a little weight by taking up jogging. Did I say the
wicker-basket faction were the worst offenders? I lied. Heaving, steaming, sweating, stinking joggers elbowing their way
through crowded pavements beat them by a jockstrap. Apart
from being antisocial they're so desperately unattractive, and
you know their flats are full of muesli and back numbers of
New Society.

Mr Myerscough offered to take me on a guided tour of

London, showing me the more blatant examples of pavement abuse, and I agreed to go to the association's offices in Vauxhall. It used to be said that all roads lead to Rome, but that was before they built the Vauxhall roundabout where the Pedestrian Association's offices are located. The roads are controlled by eleven sets of traffic lights so cunningly linked as to prevent the pedestrian ever making it beyond the third island on the right, where stands the sign inscribed Fulham, Oxford and South Wales. There was a very old and wasted man leaning against the bollard in the middle of the island, who shook his head hopelessly when I asked if he wanted any help.

I tried going down among the labyrinthine passages of the subway, but kept coming up on strangely unconnected stretches of pavement locked in by iron railings. I tried going up over a raised walkway at which the Great Wallenda himself might have quaked, so high, so narrow, so long was it and so dangerously exposed to sudden gusts. In the end I hailed a taxi and asked him to drive me to the other side of the roundabout. He didn't seem at all surprised.

Slightly touched

Strictly for health reasons I surrendered the other morning to a pleasurable sensual experience on the floor of a small tutorial room at the North East London Polytechnic's School for Independent Study, not far from West Ham Football ground. My partner in this salutary exercise (part of a controlled scientific project being undertaken by five first-year students) was a bony young man in a yellow sweatshirt called Kelly. We tried it three different ways, Kelly and I: the first was called Being Moved, the second Pushing and the third Sticking. Before each experience, he checked the correct procedure in a textbook. Without going into too much detail at this stage I can tell you that all three experiences were unequivocally tactile.

When we had finished, another young man, who had been observing us closely for the purpose of collating empirical data, handed me a bright pink badge bearing the slogan *Touch For Health Month*; enjoined me to touch three male and three female persons in the next week, observing their reactions; and wished me luck in the manner of a colonel sending a subaltern over the top. In the two hours that I have been wearing the badge I have to report that I have not yet achieved my sixfold objective but, curiously, I have had my bottom pinched seventeen times.

That's the trouble with Higher Education. The lower orders don't appreciate what you're trying to do. At the tutorial before the workshop, one of the two girl students on the project, a nubile young woman called Natalie sporting shocking-pink socks, a blue bandana and enough cowbells on her person to equip a small dairy farm, complained to the tutor that much of the testable, evaluative element of the project had been misunderstood by the Press. By touch she, of course, meant a spontaneous incident of brief manipulative pressure on someone's shoulder or arm, designed solely to raise the level of casual social interaction. But all the man from the *Daily Mirror* wanted her to do was go out and grab people's bums. And what's more, exclusively male bums. Natalie's bells tinkled indignantly.

Bob, the tutor, sympathised. He said an experiment of this nature could well throw up a lot of stuff which she had to be disciplined enough to handle and that random response to it was bound to be ambivalent. Kelly, who was sitting next to Natalie nursing on his knees a book about Tai Chi – a sort of therapeutic martial dancing – offered the opinion that Western conceptualisation of scientific validity was often stereotyped. Bob then asked Paul what reaction he had observed in the six people he had set out to touch since their last tutorial. Paul, who had a streaming cold, replied that without exception the recipients of his tactile advances had broken into a broad smile, thereby proving that the experience had relaxed them, reduced inherent tension and therefore improved their health, apart from the possible onset of a head cold.

I lost the cut and thrust of the debate for a while, for I was suddenly overwhelmed by nostalgia for the long-lost days when as an undergraduate I, too, experienced the delights of tutorials, albeit of a rather drier variety than the ones offered at the School for Independent Study. Compared to some of the degrees that these North-East Poly students were studying – Deep Sea Safety Methods, Strategies in Neuro-Linguistic Language Management Programming, History of Broderie Anglaise – Eng. Lit. was pretty small beer. We used to sit stiffly on the edges of Mr R. B. D. French's chairs surrounded by Mr R. B. D. French's leather-bound editions of George Eliot, discussing Keats's use of metaphor as dispassionately as if we were itemising the ingredients for steamed jam roll. Only on one occasion was there a momentary lapse. Mr French asked each of us to quote a stanza from memory. Self-consciously and haltingly, we all did our duty by John Masefield and Thomas Hood, and then Felicity Wallis, a Sixties precursor of the Sloane Ranger, said the only poem she could remember went thus:

In Huddersfield, in Huddersfield
There was a cow that wouldn't yield.
The reason that she wouldn't yield
She didn't like her udders feeled.

My reverie was interrupted by Kelly, who was suggesting that we had a quick run-through of the procedures for next Thursday's touch workshop which was open to the public. He wanted to try out an exercise called Slapping Into Warmth, he said, which involved beating one's partner lightly all over his/her body. But bearing in mind the possibility that one or two hacks from the *Daily Mirror* might be in attendance, he thought they might leave this one out.

Since the project started a couple of weeks before, the instances of casual social and familial touching between strangers at the School for Independent Study had increased dramatically. Last Thursday Nick had sat in the canteen for an hour and no one had touched each other. This Thursday twenty-five people had done so. If, said Nick, looking at his notes, everyone touched six people and told those six to touch six more like a sort of physical chain-letter, the odds were that in a very short time everyone in Britain would have had their level of casual social interaction raised.

On a personal note, I met the editor coming out of the Gents just now and put my arm round his shoulder. He didn't break into a broad grin, he looked nervously over his shoulder and said maybe I should see him in his office. Well, that's a healthy sign, I suppose.

Après-fish couture

'And now we have a Mrs Coulter calling us from Basingstoke. What is your question please Mrs Coulter?'

'It's my hems. I've just made this tartan skirt on the bias and I can't get the hem straight. I've tried everything.'

'Thank you Mrs Coulter. Now then Betty, what's the answer?'

'Well, first let me say how much I sympathise with Mrs Coulter. I know just what it's like to have a dip in the middle between one's legs . . .'

Heaven knows why I was listening to a phone-in programme about home dressmaking the other morning. I know absolutely nothing about dressmaking or, for that matter, any other kind of sewing. The worst moment of my life was when, having applied for a job as a supply teacher some years ago, I was dispatched to East Ham to teach Eng Lit and to my horror the headmistress showed me into a room full of sewing machines. 'But Miss Trubshaw, I don't know anything about sewing,' I began.

'No buts, Miss Arnold. Mrs Bratby is away and you will be taking over her fifteen needlework and embroidery periods.'

After a week substituting for Mrs Bratby I came to the conclusion that embroidery is to East Ham what emery boards were to King Kong – low priority. Just as well since I didn't know the difference between lazy daisy and herringbone. Fortunately most of the pupils' queries were of a less technical nature. 'Miss, I've lorst me bleedin' bobbin',,' or 'Please Miss, where's me effin' fimble?'

My misery was short-lived. By half-term most of the sewing machines had been dismantled, presumably to be reassembled in some parental sweatshop elsewhere, and stitchcraft was dropped from the curriculum.

Thus it was with mixed feelings that I opened an advanced copy of a glossy new book to be published next month called *Secrets of the Couturiers* by Frances Kennett. The point of the book is to explain to enthusiasts how they can achieve the *haute couture* look for a tenth of what they'd have to pay in Paris. Frankly, even a tenth of a Dior gown is ten times as much as I'd pay for a dress, but no matter. Last time I went to a Paris fashion show I made inquiries about a pretty slip of an evening dress and was told that it cost £3,000. 'Of course, if you were to wait until the end of the collections you could buy the actual cat-walk outfit cheaper,' they said.

'How cheap?'

'Half price.'

'Good grief. Fifteen hundred smackers for a dress that's done 10,000 miles with several oil changes to boot. No thanks.'

I said as much to Ms Kennett, who sympathised. Her book reveals the little trademarks by which every top designer is recognised – the Dior pleat, the Cardin over-stitch, the Schiaparelli tuck. Hang on, I said, aren't all those folk a bit old hat? What about the Gibb gusset and the Rhodes ruche? Ms Kennett said the classics were always touchstones from which to learn.

How does one learn this magic lore? Where else but at the London College of Fashion, just off Oxford Street, which gives diplomas in everything to do with stitchcraft. Miss Teague, head of design, told us about the syllabus and what the College looked for in young designers. A sense of colour was paramount, the ability to draw inessential. It was flair they were after and you could tell if someone had that just by looking at them. She said she would show us the students cutting, designing, drawing, embroidering, knitting.

'Surely you don't teach *knitting*?' I said, trying to visualise Madame Schiaparelli hunched over a pair of number 11s muttering purl one, knit two together.

'Not that sort of knitting – machine work,' said Miss Teague. 'We place students in some of the top international knitwear design companies. We had a student here, originally on a bespoke tailoring course, but it was obvious he had talent. The other students brought their lunch in Littlewood's carriers, Richard's was always from Fortnum's. He's with Missoni now. I believe his father was a director with Cecil Gee.'

We went to the sample room. 'Always put your pins in lengthways,' a teacher was explaining to a student who appeared to be working on the Turin Shroud. We saw all-in-one cloaks, capes and dresses which aren't called cloaks, capes and dresses, they are *garments*, sometimes even apparel. We saw some exquisite garments the students have just designed for the House of Hardy, who make upmarket fishing tackle – exquisite stitching, wonderful colours. I thought of some of the men I know who fish.

'Surely real fishermen would think these garments a little mimsy-pimsy,' I said.

'Well, they're more *après-fish*,' said Miss Teague.

I like that. I must read *Secrets of the Couturiers* more carefully. What I'm after is a subtle little garment to take me through the school run, the office, and late night shopping, a sort of *après Sainsbury's* number. Actually I think I already have one. It's called a nightie.

Scents and sensibility

It all started, as a lot of things do, on a couch in a hotel room one sunny afternoon with the curtains drawn, the door locked and most of my clothes hanging on the peg behind the door. I was, as you will have guessed, undergoing a session of aromatherapy beneath the soothing and practised hands of an attractive Frenchwoman called Danielle Ryman. Mademoiselle Ryman trained under the late Madame Marguerite Maury, the Parisian biochemist who, at the start

of this century, developed and modernised the ancient oriental art of skin rejuvenation and general physical well-being by
the use of essential oils.

It was not, I confess, my first bite at the aromatherapeutic
cherry. Some time last year my friend Melissa said, 'Do me a
favour, Sue. I know this frightfully nice girl who's just
started up in aromatherapy. Could you go along and be a
guinea-pig?'

Now my knowledge of essential oils is limited to cooking,
castor, Castrol and a curious khaki substance in a bottle
shaped like the Eiffel Tower labelled 'Huile de Bain' that my
aunt gave me for Christmas; but Melissa is not a friend to be
trifled with, so off I went. The frightfully nice girl looked me
up and down with laser eyes and then asked all sorts of deeply
personal questions about my life and times, the books I read,
the music I preferred, the food I ate and the hours I kept. She
then closed her eyes for twenty seconds and at last cried out
sharply as though she had just sat on a sea urchin, '*Sandalwood*. You *are* sandalwood. You are warm, vibrant, sen-
suous, impetuous, strong, vital, reckless and *alive*. It *has* to
be sandalwood.'

Naturally I was impressed that a stranger should have the
wit to grasp the essential Arnold on so short an acquaintance,
but my enthusiasm waned when the aromatherapist flung
open the door of a small cabinet which as far as I could see
contained only jars marked 'Sandalwood'.

So when not long ago I was again invited for a session on
the aromatic couch with Mlle Ryman, I declined. I've done
it, I said. It was like an ordinary massage only a bit smellier.
Mlle Ryman protested. I had been duped. It was ridiculous,
she said, that only sandalwood had been used, for there were
altogether 250 essential oils from flowers, plants, herbs, roots
and bark which had to be scientifically combined to give the
correct result. Only disciples of Mme Maury could know the
precise method for treating a client, for only Mme Maury and

her homeopathic doctor husband had devoted their lives to the odoriferous cause.

I looked at the price list. It was incredibly costly – £25 for instance for a small bottle of face cream. Mlle Ryman shrugged apologetically. It *was* expensive, she agreed, but it had to be so for it took a ton of rose petals to produce one kilo of essential rose oil and as for carnation, *ouf*! – at £5,700 a kilo retail, it was more expensive than gold. I felt myself warming to the idea of so much hedonism in a jar. Imagine a ton of rose petals being hand-squeezed (I had presumed they were hand-squeezed) by Bulgarian peasants just to provide a few metropolitan fat cats with a couple of pots of pong. That's the trouble with all this retrenchment and brown rice: occasionally something inside you rebels and you yearn for carnation oil at £5,700 smackers a throw. OK, I said to Mlle Ryman, I'll come along.

At university I had this friend called Josephine who, when she was seventeen, had a car accident outside Selfridges and, as a result, lost her sense of smell. Poor Jo was put through a tedious series of medical hoops to prove to the insurance hawks that she really had lost it and was finally awarded £1,700, which didn't seem a lot. She had the last laugh. A couple of years later she got it back while walking through the bazaar in Cairo. I thought of Jo when I went into Mlle Ryman's aromatherapy clinic in a West End hotel. There was such a profusion and confusion of aromas hanging in the air like wet washing that I wouldn't have been able to distinguish frangipani from Fairy Liquid. I can't remember half the ingredients Mlle Ryman claimed her oils contained but here are a few; Bulgarian rose, black pepper, basil, acacia, cactus, cypress, orange leaves, lavender, ylang ylang, cedar bark and, of course, carnation at around a fiver a drop.

'The odoriferous molecule,' she told me, 'is the only living hormone and that is why when you breathe in these fragrances they rejuvenate old worn tissue and make the body youthful.' She talked of famous French doctors with names like Gattefosse and Romanet, and described how the oils are assimilated osmotically into the skin. I think it was when she was telling me about the healing power of neroli and bergamot that I fell asleep, dreaming of drowning in cow parsley.

It must have been fate that the following week I found myself looking for somewhere to park on the Côte d'Azur. There wasn't a space – so I retreated inland from Antibes and quite suddenly I thought I was back on Miss Ryman's couch. The air was suffocatingly fragrant, one sniff and I felt I'd gulped a pint of Patou. Of course, I was driving into Grasse, perfume capital, said the banner across the road, of the world.

I stopped. Where, I asked, could I see the simple peasants handpicking the rose petals for the essential oils? Curious glances all round, but I was directed to the laboratories of a famous French perfume house. There were neither peasants nor petals. There were, however, huge vats, drums, winches and the sort of intricate pipework that you would associate more with British Leyland than bougainvillaea.

'Where are the flower petals?' I asked. 'Visitors may not visit the plantations,' snapped a guide. In the queue for the gift shop, where bottles of essential oils the size of tin tacks cost 350 francs, I stood behind two American youths in cut-off jeans and Ivy League sweatshirts.

'Hey Joe,' said one. 'Why'd you cash 200 bucks just now? We're gonna be in Italy tonight.'

'Because I gotta buy my grandmother some o' this shit, that's why,' said Joe.

Pow! Sock! Biff!

Let's see, what time is it? Coming up for midnight and a moonless night to boot. Perfect. I think I'll mosey down to Mile End swinging my bulging handbag, find a really dark alley and put in a little ju-te-do practice. The first fifteen-stone hairy who jumps me, seizing my throat with hands the size of family meat pies, I'll treat to my elbow lever, wrench and pivot trick, following on with a knuckle strike to the left ear and a couple of quick kicks in the shins. To the second sixteen-stone brute who jumps me, grasping both my wrists with hands the size of Berber water bottles, I'll offer my double up-thrust wrist jab, breaking both his thumbs. I saunter on. There is a flash of naked steel and a third assailant, 18-stone and built like a low-loader, grabs my hair with hands the size of Mexican saddlebags. He gets my fluent forehand cut (which breaks his elbow), my delicate knee in the gut and my gentle foot in the face. He retires.

I'm a little disappointed that no one has attempted to garrotte me with cheese wire, strangle me with a stocking or thrust a gun barrel between my shoulder blades, because I badly need to brush up the Tiger Claw, the Peacock Parry and the Fatal Double Palm Ancient Oriental Ear Zonk. No matter. Confucius he say better leave few kicks for new day; and, anyway, tomorrow Mr Biffin is going to teach me how to fend off rapists in tight skirts and high heels – me, not the rapists, though in order to appreciate this female problem for himself the conscientious Mr Biffin wore a tight skirt and stilettos while working out the method.

Four months ago Chris Biffin devised a unique method of self defence exclusively for women, based on his extensive knowledge of judo, karate, ju jitsu, nin jitsuc, Tein shan pai, mechanical engineering, active service with the paras in Borneo, basic common sense, and a macho-minded mother who made him take up the martial arts at the age of four. Her favourite maternal trick was to lie in wait for her treasure brandishing a broomhead wrapped in sacking with which, if he didn't watch out, she would belabour him about the ears.

He now teaches his method, entitled ju-te-do, the Way of Gentle Hands, in a west London leisure centre, and his classes are already packed out. Models, housewives, police-women, shop girls, pensioners, they're all queueing to know how to protect themselves effectively without panic and without screaming. No use screaming, says the practical Mr Biffin, no one will help and it takes your mind off the job. After one lesson I can vouch for its effectiveness. I have since been round the office asking my heftier male colleagues to assault me. Some are still whimpering in the Gents.

What baffles me is why some bright young TV producer hasn't signed up Mr Biffin, who is young, articulate and personable, for a Teach Yourself Self Defence series. It would literally be a knockout, entertaining, instructive, a real public service. I suppose they're far too busy working on those Teach Yourself Knitting and Sheep Dog Grooming blockbusters.

The basis of his method is leverage. There is no point in a woman trying to grapple with an opponent on a deltoid-for-deltoid level. She must outwit him which, of course, isn't difficult as she's better endowed in that department already. Thus if the thug throttles you from the back you lean back against him using his strength to help you while you whip both hands behind you and grab his groin in a Tiger Claw. 'If you've got his bag of sweets in a vice he's not going to bother you for long,' said Mr Biffin, who has a colourful turn of phrase.

He also has a useful line against rush-hour gropers and party octopuses, which he calls his Casanova technique. I wish I'd known about it last week when I was sitting on top of the number 22 cruising along Piccadilly, happily engrossed in *The Siege of Krishnapur*. The man sitting beside me suddenly gripped my thigh and started a slow rhythmic massage. I feebly shifted further away and got off at the next stop. Now I could have given him a quick knuckle jab paralysing his fingers, or even the Little Finger Wrench, which never fails and leaves the victim in a state of mental collapse.

That's the endearing thing about Mr Biffin. He doesn't merely get the attacker off your back, he advises you to finish him off. Immobilise him, tie him up with your Hermès scarf, and *then* call the police. Mr Biffin – Biff to friends – is in demand to demonstrate his methods in girls' schools and women's groups. I think I'll finish the beginner's course and then book a winter break on the New York waterfront. Practice makes perfect.

Memory lane

Largely because I had £1.26 in my purse, which didn't allow much slack for a tip, I decided to engage the taxi driver in amiable conversation. 'Do you know,' I began, leaning forward in friendly fashion and all but knocking out my teeth on the glass partition, 'I'm going to see this amazing hypnotherapist who can take you back to your former incarnations.'

'Not that geezer from Liverpool what does regressions and such – Joe Soap or summink,' said the taxi driver.

'Well, yes, as a matter of fact,' I said, a bit deflated. 'Joe Keeton actually. What do you know about regression and reincarnation?'

'Not a lot. I'm more into meditation myself – that Indian bloke with the 'uge country-style mansion. Went up there last April and did a course in transcendental meditation. I do it in the back of me cab twice a day. Bloody fantastic. Changed me life,' said the taxi driver, carving up a woman in a green Volvo.

Mr Keeton's persuasive powers are the subject of a book, *Encounters With The Past* published by Sidgwick and Jackson (£7.95). In simple terms Mr Keeton places his subjects under deep hypnosis, instructs them to go back in time to a certain year, say 1876, and, hey presto, they will apparently assume the identity of a contemporaneous character, a monk, a midwife, a midshipman. No fantasy, no imagination, says Mr Keeton, just pure memory. Now my mother, being half Burmese, is a great believer in pagoda-power and reincarnation, so I thought I'd give it a whirl.

I arrived just in time for the delivery, at least that's what it sounded like. In a large hotel room full of people drinking wine a woman was screaming rhythmically, as in those B-films where the doctor keeps calling for 'plenty of hot water'. But no, it was not childbirth, it was merely one of Mr Keeton's subjects, a homely young woman in a pink cardigan, being regressed. Instead of being a plain Scottish lexicographer called Sue, she was now a turn-of-the-century urchin who'd just been kicked by a horse.

Mr Keeton sat in a chair next to Sue, alias Charlie murmuring soothingly. He was a short, bearded, bulky figure whose jacket barely buttoned round his girth. He looked exactly as you'd imagine, say, the catering manager of the *Liverpool Post* to look, which is precisely what he is. When not ordering bushels of processed peas, Mr Keeton lectures on ESP, practises hypnotherapy and regresses people. For free.

'Drift off, Charlie, drift away, feel no pain,' murmured Mr Keeton.

'Now, has anyone else got a date they want Sue to regress to?'

'1492 please,' I called out.

'Now then, Sue,' said Mr Keeton, 'I want you to take your memory back to the year 1942 – it *is* the year 1942, who are you, where are you?'

'Not 1942, *1492*,' snapped Mr Keeton's wife Monica, who jangled when she moved.

'Sorry, 1492 – who are you?'

Sue started twisting restlessly in her chair, her pink cardigan rumpled, she began panting. I though she might foam at the mouth. Sue suddenly opened her mouth, gurgled hoarsely and started tugging at her tongue.

'What's happening, what is she doing?' I asked in fright.

'She is telling us that she is a mute. Drift off, Sue, it is now the year 1765. Who are you, where are you, what are you doing?'

'I am Father Anthony Bennet, I am praying in my chapel . . .' began Sue the Scottish lexicographer, alias Charlie the urchin, alias the medieval mute, alias Bob's your uncle.

For the rest of the evening we put Sue through her reincarnationary paces. She seemed particularly keen on portraying teenage girls doing wrong in turnip fields or small blasphemous boys. More often than not when asked for a specific historic fact like 'Who is on the throne,' she would mutter incoherently, laugh insanely or be rescued by Mr Keeton telling her to drift off to another date.

Mr Keeton said that many of the 'facts' revealed by his subjects could be verified. Others, such as whether there was really a mute living somewhere in the world in 1492, could not.

Afterwards Mr Keeton put volunteers into deep hypnotic states. 'Go on, have a go,' said a girl friend who has tried it and now falls into a trance every time Mr Keeton says the special catch phrase.

'No thanks,' I said, and headed purposefully toward a deep hypnotic double scotch.

Pink-washing the British budgie

On Tuesday I went to a Press briefing, drank three glasses of pink champagne and made a shopping list – to wit:

One budgerigar (anaemic)
One birdcage (cheap)
One bottle Ribena
Suitable quantities shrimps, prawns, carrots, rhubarb, beet-root etc . . .

'Allow me to refresh your glass,' said a girl in rose-coloured spectacles, 'and may I introduce you to Arthur Hissey, resident budgerigar consultant?'

Mr Hissey, an elegant figure sporting a candy-coloured carnation in his buttonhole, sat down on the sofa.

'Ah, Mr Hissey,' I said, 'about this £1,000 cash prize for the first genuine pink budgerigar . . .'

Allow *me* to refresh your memories. Fifteen years ago

97

Britain's biggest birdseed manufacturer offered a £500 reward to anyone who could produce a pink budgie. There were a number of false alarms which sent Mr Hissey chasing round the country to inspect salmon, cerise and even shocking-pink birds, all of which subsequently failed the soap and water test. Every so often a traveller would return from the uncharted areas of Exmoor or Erith or East Sheen with reports of another pink-plumed budgie, related in the wild-eyed raving manner of explorers talking about the Yeti, but nothing more was heard. This year the birdseed sponsors doubled the stakes.

'Why,' I asked Mr Hissey, having listened in some confusion to his talk of genetic pigmentation, 'do you specifically want a *pink* one? Why not black or khaki?'

'Come now,' said Mr Hissey, spreading his hands, 'pink is such a charming shade. Just imagine a pair of pink birds in a gilded cage in an elegant London drawing room. Pure enchantment. Interior decorators would go wild.'

I tried to imagine it, but all I could see was a thousand smackers in used notes stacked neatly in a battered attaché case. 'How likely is it that anyone will produce a pink budgie simply by working out the genetic combinations scientifically?' I said.

'It's impossible,' said Mr Hissey. 'The only way it will happen is by accident. A fluke. A one-off mutation.'

We'll see about that, I thought, and contacted the genetics expert at London Zoo. 'I was just wondering,' I began guardedly (no point in showing my hand at this stage), 'how you manage to keep your flamingoes so healthy, so blooming, so *pink*?'

'Carotenoids,' said the expert.

'Carotewhats?'

'Pink food colouring. Shrimps, for instance, turn flamingoes pink. We used to give them shrimps but it got too expensive, so we give them a pellet containing carotin. We do the same for scarlet ibis and rainbow trout. Years ago we used to use a chemical called canthaxanthin made in Switzerland. Trouble was they didn't send the instructions and I think we overdosed them. The flamingoes turned a rather violent puce.'

'This canthaxanthin,' I said, trying to keep my voice casual . . . 'D'you think it would work on budgies?'

'No. The pigment that colours budgerigar feathers works by a different process.'

'One last thing. Would it be possible to cross a flamingo, a very, very small one of course, with a large budgie?'

'Certainly not. Different species.'

Tuesday evening saw me heading north to Tottenham, home of Mr Frank Warren, well-known breeder of prize-winning birds. Mr Warren showed me magnificent violet budgies which had won Best In Show blue ribbons, and extraordinary emerald budgies for which he had refused £400 apiece, and resplendent azure budgies which strutted about their cages like emperors and disdained to emit a single cheep.

'How would you go about breeding a pink one?' I said.

'I wouldn't. I breed for quality not for gimmicks. Besides, you couldn't do it scientifically. It'd be a fluke.'

I played my last card. I telephoned the Natural History Museum.

'Why do robins have red breasts?' I asked. 'They don't eat shrimps, do they?'

'No, but robins aren't really red. That's just for romantics and Christmas cards. It's more a sort of dirty brick colour . . .'

I think I'll stick to Ribena.

Many years ago I lived rent-free in a magnificent penthouse in Rome while the owners were abroad, on the one condition, said the estate agent sternly, that I watered the plants. Amazed at my good fortune, I arrived at Piazza Mazzini to discover 157 occupied flower pots, tubs, urns, boxes and baskets on the front terrace and, after I had hacked my way into it, a small tropical jungle at the back. Every room was crowded with vegetation crying out for nourishment. The agent handed me a dossier of instructions and departed. It took three hours a day to feed the flowers, and when I left I knew the Italian for John Innes compost and 'Why is my gloxinia drooping?'

It was, therefore, with bitter-sweet nostalgia that I read a letter the other day from a lady in Belgravia, on rose-pink writing paper with a rose pinned to the bottom, inviting me to see a unique new conception in three-dimensional flower living and her automatic plant-watering system. Now, I am as interested as anyone in three-dimensional flower living, but I must confess it was the automatic plant-watering system that lured me to Miss Jeanette Norell's gracious five-storey home in Elizabeth Street. Miss Norell is perhaps better known for her Grooming and Deportment Consultancy, where she gives advice on such problems as foundation garments, ascent and descent of stairs, how to receive business clients, and superfluous hair. Three-dimensional flora is a new venture.

Miss Norell has converted the ground floor of her house

into a silk-flower boutique and it was here, attractively
framed in a rose bower, that she was standing when I arrived.
It was a very nice bower. It was interwoven with tiny
hand-made rosebuds and threaded with fairy lights; and as
well as being an attractive place in which to stand framed
occasionally, it is also hired out by Miss Norell for weddings,
christenings, diplomatic receptions – any occasion, in fact,
where an illuminated rose bower is a must.

I admired the hand-made silk gladioli from Brussels and
the machine-made polyester ivy from Taiwan (recommended for kitchens and bathrooms, and more in my price
range), and Miss Norell told me she had represented Great
Britain for many years in flower-arranging competitions. She
had studied the art in Japan, which makes her a green belt, I
suppose.

We then made an extended tour of the house. I followed
Miss Norell, a statuesque woman who clearly practises what
she preaches about foundation garments, up the stairs, eager
to see how a consultant in grooming and deportment herself
tackles this problem. She did it superbly – smooth, sure-
footed, head erect and with the third and fourth fingers
lightly touching the banisters.

What exactly is three-dimensional flower living, I wondered, ducking to avoid an overhanging bough of bougainvil-
lea. 'Flowers everywhere,' said my hostess, 'real where
possible, silk where not and Natural Vistas at every window.'
She showed me. There were silk, polyester, pearlised, plastic, metal and dried flowers in the rooms. Clusters of fantasy
frangipani dangled dangerously over the master bed, boughs
of forsythia and fuchsia o'er-canopied the dining-table. The
window boxes were awash with blooms, and out of every
unlikely window, such as utility room and lavatory, where
you might expect to see pipes and dustbins and empty milk
bottles, there were Natural Vistas. Somehow Miss Norell
had positioned lichen-covered boulders from Cumbria,

craggy rocks from Scotland and expensive acrylic spruces (essential because of the lack of light) on slabs of concrete and guttering. It was all quite extraordinary.

'Extraordinary, quite extraordinary,' I murmured, 'but will you show me your automatic watering system?'

My hostess indicated a control panel to which every window box, flower pot and Natural Vista was connected and programmed. At a given time every day, according to season, light density and atmospheric pressure, water in the form of drip mist is fed into the boxes. 'Nowhere better,' said Miss Norell, leading the way down stairs, 'could this be demonstrated than in the basement fern cave and grotto.'

Down we went, smooth, sure-footed, and in the small open space just below the pavement a plethora of wondrous ferns in all shapes and sizes and hues and pots greeted us. A small tree in the corner of the grotto looked a little off-colour, I thought, but Miss Norell was busy explaining how the expensive American automatic-watering system also included special growing strip-lights.

We stood in the grotto admiring the ferns and then, suddenly, inexplicably, for this was high noon and no time for drip mist, a steady trickle of water began falling from above. Upon the withered tree it fell, and even upon Miss Norell herself. She looked at her watch, confused. Had the system failed? We both looked up to determine the source of the water. A large black labrador was cocking its leg over the pavement railings.

'Oh, oh, oh, go away, you brute!' cried Miss Norell. 'No wonder my poor little tree is dying. Just wait till I find its owner. It's really too much.'

We left the fern cave and grotto, plotting vengeance. There are, it seems, cheaper automatic plant-watering systems on the market.

Word power

Another week, another story, another mental block – I wonder if I should get a word processor and revolutionise my life? Travelling home in the rush hour the other evening, I found myself locked in an involuntary clinch with a young middle manager (anyone who smells of aftershave at 5.30 pm must be in middle management because it shows they're really *keen*). I do not normally relish this kind of gratuitous intimacy on the District Line, but on this occasion I scarcely noticed his waistcoat buttons jammed against my ribcage, so fascinated was I by what he was saying to an invisible companion over his shoulder.

'Word processors cut out all the routine drudgery of typing,' he said. 'They're fast, efficient and error-free. They have memories, they store information like a computer and they can give you a pageful of facts at the touch of a button.'

'Coo, can they really?' said the invisible friend, female. 'I bet they don't come cheap.'

'You can hire them in shops by the hour,' said the young middle manager. 'You take in a rough draft and they write the stuff for you. But that's not the half of it . . .'

I never heard the other half because they got out at the next stop. Strange fantasies began to form in my mind. I saw myself first thing every Monday morning going down to the word processing shop, sitting in front of a small machine, my handbag on my lap, and saying politely, 'A thousand words on tattooed ladies please. Oh, and can you keep it fairly clean? It's for a family newspaper.'

Chug, whirr, click, goes the word processor obediently, and two minutes later (they print at 500 words a minute you know) out comes next Sunday's column – straight margins, correct spelling, ready-checked facts. 'Thanks a lot,' I say pressing sundry banknotes into its tabulator. 'See you next week.'

Two days later I found myself attending a large, lavish Press reception to launch the first word-processing bureau franchise in Britain. It was one of those lecture-first, booze-later affairs, and when I arrived a man in cavalry twills who looked like the Group Head Sales Development and Marketing Manager (UK) was talking enthusiastically about 3 per cent market penetration. I was handed a sheaf of information, a clip-board, a note book, a silver ballpoint, a glass of wine and an ashtray, and shown to a seat.

Word processors are to typewriters what telephones are to pigeons, the Group Head Sales and Development Manager (UK) was saying. Word processors were revolutionising office life. The franchise scheme was ideally suited to the married woman in her 30s with previous secretarial experience looking to resume her career at a higher level and also provide the family with a second income.

'Does that mean the money's so lousy you couldn't live on it as your *only* income,' shouted a hack at the back. Reporters can be very rude.

'Not at £13.50 an hour which is the going rate to hire one,' said the man next to me. 'You could make a fortune in a prime City site.'

I will not dwell on the franchise angle, not because I didn't quite understand it, but because my principal reason for coming was to see this miracle of high tech in action. Straight after the speeches, and nobly resisting *vol au vents* and Veuve de Vernay, I made my way to the silent row of word processors which looked like ordinary electric typewriters with a few extra keys and a small video screen where the paper would normally be.

'What can it do?' I asked the bearded young demonstrator.

'Anything you like. What do you want it to do?'

'Write stories.'

'Stories? You mean reports, letters, legal documents, contracts, menus, programmes.'

'No, stories like once upon a time there was an elephant . . .'

The bearded young man looked doubtful, then brightened.

'Say you wanted to research all the stories written about elephants from April 1976 to August 1980 and send out 1,000 copies to various clients. You'd insert the relevant elephant-story disc, like putting a cassette on a tape, punch a few keys and there it is on the screen . . . see. Now, say you realised you didn't want any reference to *Indian* elephants when you'd written the report. You'd just press the erase button and all the Indian elephants would go and the rest of the report would remain intact – no rubbing out or re-typing.'

'You mean it's like a mechanical rubber,' I said.

'Yes – er – that is, of course not, it's much more complicated than that.'

Slowly, sadly, the light was beginning to dawn. If Shakespeare had had a word processing bureau up the road from the Globe, he could have inserted the Scottish Murders disc, rejigged all the relevant info and sent 1,000 copies off to various agents, asking if there was any chance of an advance on this play he was thinking of writing called 'Macbeth'. Then he'd have had to get out the old quill and parchment and inspiration and get down to writing it. It's the old story. You only get out what you put in.

Heavy-hearted, I returned to the *vol au vents*. It's not a word processor I need, it's a Muse who can type.

'Ho ho ho,' boomed a fruity voice behind me, and a hand the size of a chump chop clapped me on the shoulder. 'I know just what you're looking for. Come with me, I'm your Uncle Holly.' Vaguely wondering how on earth Uncle Holly could have known I was looking for Ladies' Dressing Gowns, but happy to find any form of deliverance from the bedlam that overtakes Selfridges at this time of year, I turned and saw a huge man with a disturbing resemblance to a Toby jug, dressed in a bright green frock coat and breeches. His nose, cheeks and chin were scarlet and he carried a cane.

'This way, this way. Follow me everyone,' cried Uncle Holly spreading his huge arms, and like some great trawler he gathered up in his wake a shoal of little sprats in bobble caps and woolly scarves and anoraks with E.T. on the back, and school parties headed by harassed-looking teachers, and mothers with prams, and old ladies with carrier bags. And me. 'This way to the Magic Grotto and a visit to Father Christmas. Uncle Nigel will give you all a nice Paddington Bear badge on your way in. Come along. Ho ho ho.'

We had reached a fenced-off area from which unseen voices were singing 'Silent Night'. Uncle Nigel was not wearing breeches or a frock coat. He was dressed with the usual glum anonymity of a store detective and he threw Uncle Holly a bitter look. I tried to extricate myself from the mob but it was impossible. With the handle of a push chair jammed into my back I was pitched forward into the grotto. Somewhere up the line a child had begun to shriek rhythmically, uncontrollably, unnervingly, like someone having a tooth drawn without anaesthetics.

'What's the matter, Jasper? It's only Paddington sawing a piece of wood.'

'Please, Miss Picton, he's crying because he's dropped his bug scrammer and Gary Trotter's gone and trod on it.'

There were twelve animated tableaux of Paddington Bear getting into all sorts of saucy scrapes. The adults appeared to relish the little fellow's antics far more than the kids, who glanced briefly at the sets and then pushed restlessly on.

'Oh, do look children. Paddington's trying to mend a burst pipe in his red wellies. Isn't he *sweet*?'

'What's so sweet about a stupid old bear? My bruvver's class went to the London Dungeon last week. Said it was triff. People getting their stomachs eaten out by real rats and people getting tortured, and all.'

'Kevin, Samantha, Jade, Natasha, Digby, wait here with Miss Wiltshire while I take the others to see Santa.'

Father Christmas was waiting for us by the Exit sign. He was sitting sideways on his stool like a man who is giving one buttock a rest. His boots were snowy white and his face had a waxy look about it as if he needed fresh air. He probably does. He's been on grotto shift since the end of October. One by one the children were pushed forward, often with reluctance, to shake the saint's hand. To each he put the same two questions and the answers came pat: 'Hayley. And I want one of those dolls that drinks milk and wets itself.' Or: 'William, and I'm getting a snooker table.'

If a child refused to identify itself Father Christmas would pat its head in a weary, patient, understanding way and guide it firmly towards the door. Every so often he lifted one white gloved hand in a pontifical gesture and murmured 'Merry Christmas,' faintly, almost sadly.

Outside the crowds had thickened. Uncle Holly was having to marshal the grotto visitors into groups with his malacca cane. 'Where are the reindeer if he comes from Greenland every day?' asked a child suspiciously.

'Uncle Nigel's got them safe in their stable.'

'Who's Uncle Nigel?'

'He's my friend,' said Uncle Holly.

Uncle Nigel said something under his breath and passed the children over to Auntie Joy.

'Zoe, Jemima, Ben, Clarke, Portland and Dickon, wait with Miss Wiltshire while I take the others to see all the nice shiny decorations. We're not going to buy anything, just look.'

'Why can't we buy anything?'

'Because it's nice just to look, Camilla, that's why.'

On my way to Ladies' Dressing Gowns I saw a fat boy in an astrakhan coat sitting in a toy Ferrari. 'How does it work?' asked his father.

'It has a proper motor.'

'How much is it?'

'Fifteen hundred pounds.'

'I'll take two.'

Rural Rides

For deer life

At twenty to four Herr Harold shot his first Scottish stag. I didn't actually witness the historic event for I was lying in a bog behind a rock further up the hillside wrapped against the bitter north-east wind in Herr Harold's father's loden coat which came down past my wellies and up past my ears. My position afforded an unimpeded view of the magnificent purple, crimson and gold hills overlooking Glen Orchy, of the river winding far below me from Glencoe, and of Herr Harold's lederhosened backside waiting patiently for the stag to come into shot.

Thus had it been for the past hour and more, we – myself and the other non-shooting member of the stalking party – shivering aloft, they – Herr Harold and Mr Calum McFarlane Barrow the stalker – quivering below. It was better this way; Calum had said, for if we all crawled too close the deer might be disturbed and run off, which would be very sad for Herr Harold.

As it turned out Herr Harold was very happy. I daresay the stag was a bit upset, but then it hadn't driven twenty-one hours nonstop from Frankfurt or paid £100 for a day's shooting.

'What are they doing now?' I asked for the umpteenth time, moving into a drier patch of bog. My companion had the binoculars. 'Exactly the same. Harold is looking along the barrel of his rifle, Calum is looking through his telescope.'

'How much longer will it be?'

'Listen, the stag may be lying down, or even asleep. We could be here for hours yet. Stop moaning.'

Deerstalking is so exciting. I suppose technically I was only deer-stalker-stalking but it was still exciting. It had started early that morning at Craig Lodge, Dalmally – three hunters (German and Italian – 80 per cent of the shooting in Scotland these days is done by Europeans), two stalkers, two observers and an Argocat – an extraordinary vehicle, part-pram part-tank, high tech's answer to the pony. Everyone looked the part. Calum was Harris tweed throughout, including moustache. Harold, with his haversack and knitted hat, looked like a Hummel miniature come to life. When he opened his mouth I knew he was going to say '*Val de ra ha-ha-ha-ha*'. I was totally adrift in jeans that showed up like flares among the autumn tints, squeaky anorak and no hat. Nothing would send the deer flying quicker than a round pink face looming over the crest of a hill, said Calum, so I'd better bring up the rear.

First target practice. If they don't hit it, they don't go out. Of the three licensed killers, Harold is the most dead-eyed. The others head for Fasnacloich with its 2,000 deer population thirty miles west. We drive east along the river, past fishermen casting for salmon, to the estate where Calum has shooting rights over 40,000 acres. He knows there are five big stags on Forestry land, and if Harold doesn't get them the government boys will round them up and finish them off. Culling is essential, he says; there are too many deer. Far better a quick clean bullet than a lingering death from starvation through the winter.

We leave the Land-Rover and start walking silently, steadily and single file. We cross the first burn and I discover my wellies leak. We climb the first hill and I discover my soles are like glass. I quickly master the art of running on my knees, and when the others stop to spy with their field glasses I have a chance to catch up. We climb up hills and down the other side and up and up again, but we see no stags. We see buzzards swooping, and golden eagles hovering, and does with huge, sad, limpid eyes and soft white ears, and black-cock droppings which make Harold strangely agitated, but no stags. Calum says the wind is making them lie down. If we see a buck Harold should shoot; it may bring out the stags.

'If you please no buck,' says Harold. 'In Germany we are having the buck, the pig and the chicken for shooting. I wish for the stag only.'

We have our lunch at two o'clock on a hill looking down along the glen. It is indescribably, awe-inspiringly, mind-blowingly beautiful. For all you can see or hear or smell, civilisation might not exist. There is no road, no plane, no wire, no pole, no pylon, only mile after mile of fiery hillside. Harold offers me a cup cake.

'You are optimistic for my stag?' he asks Calum.

'Don't worry. We will find one,' says the trusty stalker.

Calum recently took some Belgians stalking. They packed it in after a day because they said it was too difficult; they were hunters not *Alpinistes*.

The wind has risen. My loden coat fills up with air and threatens to take off. I am beginning to sympathise with the Belgians. Calum stops, stiffens and gestures for silence. He has seen the stag. This is where you came in.

'What are they doing now?'

'Exactly the same. No, wait. Good grief, it looks like something from *Deliverance*. Calum is on all fours; Harold is kneeling over him. Oh, I see, he's resting his gun on Calum's back.' BANG.

The stag is lying in a hollow lined with emerald moss, its legs in the air like a puppy asking to be tickled. Its head is thrown back, its eyes stare, and a pair of magnificent ten-pointed antlers rear up from the mud.

'You will please take a picture,' says Harold. 'But why is your friend weeping. She is sad for the stag, *ja*?'

'Don't look now for heaven's sake,' says my companion, 'Calum is about to gralloch it.'

Back at the lodge, Calum pours octuple malt whiskies, Harold is blooded, and we gather round the piano in the lounge.

'Are you happy Harold?' I ask.

'Not so happy like Happy Birthday, but I am satisfied,' he says, and starts playing 'God Save The Queen' *fortissimo*.

Down to a sunless sea

I know a place where the sun always shines, where you can surf in a warm blue lagoon, sip Campari on a palm fringed island listening to live Hawaiian music, watch laughing children play with friendly elephants and octopuses, ogle suntanned nymphets basking on the rocks – and all, I should add, within two hours of Manchester. It's called Rhyl.

Not *Rhyl*, you cry? Not Rhyl on the north Wales coast, cheek by jowl by fish and by chip with Prestatyn and Colwyn Bay? Not rain-washed Rhyl, bastion of the boarding house and bingo hall, knee-deep in pushchairs, awash with ice lollies, where everything, even the sarnies, comes with chips and where it isn't the sun that makes you change colour, it's the dirty postcards (Matron to Nurse coming out of ward carrying saucepan, 'No no, Nurse Fanshaw, I said prick his boil')? Not *that* Rhyl?

Indeed sir, the same. I have just returned from Rhyl and bring joyful and welcome news of a daring, a dazzling, an extraordinary and wildly successful new device called the

Sun Centre. Come, take off your galoshes and I will tell you all.

It's slap on the prom past the amusement arcade called Loads of Mischief and the shoe shop called Soled Out. It looks like an Olympic greenhouse, it sounds like the Tower of Babel, and it feels like a night in Casablanca since it is kept at a constant temperature of 90F. I think it's what they call a leisure concept. If you live in Rotherham or Swindon you'll know what I mean, for Rotherham and Swindon, market leaders both in leisure concepts, have similar pleasure palaces, though not of course as marvellous.

Rhyl's free-form, glass-fibre lagoon with its surf/wave-making machine is the only one in Europe. The elephant and octopus are giant plastic water chutes, the Hawaiian singers come from Welshpool, and the nymphets owe their bronzed limbs to a row of sunbeds hard by the fat lady on the door of the women's lavatory and the gift kiosk. Fifty p in the slot, three sessions of ultra-violet coverage, and you could easily have spent a week in Palma Nova. The palm trees and the smiles on the cashiers' faces are real.

The wonderful thing about the Sun Centre is that you don't have to bother with the *real* sun at all. The day I went was one of the hottest this year, 80 degrees plus and the famous golden sands of north Wales positively crying out for occupation but lying instead lonely and litterless. Contemptuous of Apollo's gifts, six thousand happy holiday makers had raced to Kubla's plastic pleasure dome at 9 a.m., eager to pay £1.40 entrance for fourteen hours of uninterrupted, push-button hedonism. They may not have been eating lotuses but by golly they were putting away the fillets of plaice.

I was shown round by the local entertainments director, Ron Smith, an infectiously enthusiastic fellow who is constantly dreaming up schemes to attract even more tourists into the town. Why, only the other day he had this brilliant wheeze to fill the municipal swimming baths with ten thousand trout which the tourists could fish for, using painless barbless plastic-coated hooks. Feeling slightly giddy with the heat but quickly adjusting to the smell of chlorine, nicotine and chips, I passed through bevies of sparsely clad, good humoured folk to the overhead monorail from which we could get an aerial impression of the whole shebang.

We floated over the surfers (Mr Smith said he could ride the surf from one end of the lagoon to the other), we passed on to the children's splashpool where the tinies were queuing for the pink elephant chute, we flew over the island restaurant which in last year's short season of a hundred days sold fourteen tons of potato chips, we glided over the radio-controlled grand prix circuit, the swimsuit shop, ice-cream kiosks, postcard stalls, snackbars. Mr Smith said it was his considered opinion that Sun Centres were the modern equivalent of Victorian piers. I mopped the perspiration from my brow and whispered that I needed a drink. Mr Smith helped me out of the monorail carriage and said all the Sun Centre staff got drinks every hour because of de-hydration.

So there you have it. The beach brought indoors with not a grain of irritating sand to get between your toes, not a ray of real sun or a drop of real sea-water. Even the air in the Sun Centre is re-cycled and pumped back into the building.

We drove back through Snowdonia. The sun glinted over the valleys, the rivers burbled over the rocks, the air was sweet with heather. I wonder if Mr Smith could bring mountains indoors. So much more convenient.

Brighton – the naked truth

Nothing kindles the fires of pious self-righteousness better than a brisk walk after a large Sunday lunch, particularly if the day is cold, wet and generally what the Scots describe as dreich. Under these circumstances, my mother and I set out for a bracing walk along Brighton beach last Sunday. It was bitterly cold. The flags over the marina were stretched taut and swirls of mist hung from the sky like sheets flapping on an imaginary washing line.

'Good heavens,' said my mother suddenly. 'See that man on the jetty. I do believe he's *one of them*,' and she screwed up her eyes and peered intently out to sea.

With my appalling eyesight I could barely make out a jetty let alone anyone on it, but I knew exactly what she meant by *one of them*. Some years ago a small stretch of Brighton beach opposite Sussex Square was designated a naturist zone – naturist being the modern word for what we used to call nudist. I defy anyone to have spotted a Chieftain tank at that distance and in those conditions, but my mother could spot a naturist on a moonless night with a sack over her head. When the zone was proposed she had attempted to get a reduction in her rates for 'loss of amenity'.

'What amenity?' I asked.

'Not being able to take Lucy for a walk along the beach any more of course,' she replied, Lucy being her dog.

'Why can't Lucy go on the beach any more?'

'Don't be ridiculous. I couldn't expose her to that.'

It reminded me of that story about the little old lady who

telephoned the police and asked an officer to come round immediately because the man in the house opposite was behaving most indecently. A constable was dispatched forthwith and followed the little old lady up to her bedroom. 'Right then, ma'am, where is this naughty chap?' he said, cheerfully.

'There,' she said pointing outside.

'But I can't see a thing.'

'Of course you can't from *there*. But if you climb on this chest of drawers and look through a telescope . . .'

'Are you sure it's *one of them* mother?' I said. 'I mean, it's fearfully cold. Surely no one in their right mind would swim today.'

'They're not in their right minds,' said my mother triumphantly. 'That's the whole point. Look at him making an exhibition of himself. It isn't natural.'

At that moment the little train that shuttles to and fro along the beach trundled past with a few diehards in woolly balaclavas aboard. Someone pointed to the jetty and they all craned their necks.

'You must be able to see him now, Susan.'

'No, I can't.'

'Well, we'll get a little closer,' said my mother quickening her pace. 'Hurry before he goes home.' She started running across the pebbles and I stumbled after her. There was a dip and then a little rise and when we topped the rise I could see the jetty quite clearly. There was no one on it.

'Bother, he's gone,' said my mother, scanning the horizon with a disappointed air. 'Oh wait a minute, there he is, crouching behind that windbreak – see,' and she indicated a small canvas elevation like a deckchair on its side. 'I can see his feet sticking out.'

Minutes later a grey-haired man wearing nothing but a pinched expression stood up behind the screen and strode purposefully towards the water's edge. He smiled when he passed us and I said, 'You must be awfully cold.'

'I certainly am,' he replied pleasantly. 'You must think me bonkers but I promised myself a swim before the month was out.' He dipped a toe in the water. 'Ooh,' he said, 'it's absolutely freezing. My wife was right not to come.'

'Have you come far?' I said.

'From Seaford,' he said, hugging his arms round his chest to keep warm. The toy-town train clickety-clacked past again and several passengers leaned out and waved and shouted things.

'Do you mind people staring?' I said.

'No, I've got used to it. On the whole people are very reasonable. Of course it's different in the South of France. We go camping there every year. It's expensive but they've got everything, bars, sporting facilities.'

Many years ago I visited a naturist camp near Orpington and vividly recall a mixed doubles tennis match where the players were wearing only socks and gym shoes. Afterwards I went for a drink in the bar, where naked women sat on high stools with handbags over their arms. The barmaid was also starkers, she was about fifty. When she gave me my Guinness, she let out a small shriek. 'Ooh, I think I've trodden on a drawing pin.'

'You're not barefoot, are you Shirley?' someone said.

'I can't help it, I've lost my flip flops,' said Shirley.

The man from Seaford was saying that he took up naturism about ten years ago. From the corner of my eye (for I was staring fixedly at his face as we spoke) I noticed something rather odd. With one deft movement I switched my gaze from his face to his feet. They were bright orange like a Muscovy duck's.

'Why are your feet orange?' I asked.

'I think I trod in some dye up there on those stones,' he

said. 'Look, I'm going to abandon this – my wife will be waiting.'

'Are all your family naturists?' I asked.

'Only my wife. My daughter is a bit prim. She lives in Copenhagen. Well, goodbye then.'

He returned to his windshield and my mother, who had been studying a notice saying 'Keep Britain Tidy' for the last fifteen minutes, returned. 'Well, what was he like?' she asked.

'Very nice,' I said.

My mother sniffed. 'I think we'd better go home for tea,' she said.

The plot thickens

This week sees an exciting new departure for me. Without assistance from advance publicity, television advertising or a six-figure budget, I am launching my own series complete with topical tips, special offers and interviews with celebrities. I'm not sure how many weeks it will run. It all depends on the special offers. This week's is an attractive, easy care, ready-to-assemble strawberry tub which will enhance patio, terrace and balcony as well as providing you with pounds of delicious soft fruit. It should have fifty strawberry plants to go with it, but unfortunately they died.

I'd better come clean. I sent away for the wretched thing myself last year, having spied an ad which said: 'Grow your own strawberries for a tenth of the normal price – no weeding, no bending, no messing about with straw or nets or slug pellets. Each tub comes with fifty healthy plants which will yield up to 5lb of fruit each.' If you work that out as I eventually did, it makes 250lb of strawberries by mid-June. I sent away for the tub which cost £16, and thought seriously about renting a cow during Wimbledon week to provide me with cream.

The parcel arrived, a large flat oblong package which did not bode well. How do you pack a rustic wooden tub into a flat oblong package?

It was not a rustic wooden tub. It was eight livid green plastic panels with holes which you slotted together to produce something that looked like a livid green plastic dustbin with holes in it. In a separate polythene bag came the fifty plants which, said the instructions, you stuck in the holes.

The idea of getting 250lbs of strawberries from my perforated dustbin was akin to asking two glow-worms to illuminate St Paul's, but never mind. Acorns from oaks etc. I assembled the panels, filled the inside with earth, planted the plants and waited.

By the end of April, ten of my plants had mysteriously died. I say mysteriously because those plants were watched over with the tenderness of a Pietà. I washed the leaves with milk, sprayed them with bottled Malvern spa water, I *talked* to them. By the end of May, twenty-two of my precious plants had perished, and others were fading fast. To cut a long and distressing saga short, the result of my £16 investment was that by the time Mr McEnroe walked out on to the Centre Court I had two strawberries in my tub. One was small and hard and orange like a carrot, the other was misshapen, purple on one side and oddly albino on the other. No matter. They were strawberries and I had grown them. I resolved to save them for the men's final, and bought Cornish cream in anticipation of the feast.

On Saturday morning I went forth to harvest my crop. Ah me. Both the strawberries had gone. The carrot had been knocked off and run over by a child's tricycle. The albino had vanished, and to judge by the tell-tale signs a predatory greenfinch, nuthatch or water wagtail was the culprit. But I digress.

You have doubtless guessed by now that this is Part One of the Arnold Guide to Better Gardening. I'm sorry I spent so much time on the special offer. (Incidentally the tub, as new, is yours for the price of an s.a.e.) I'll race on to the interview with Mr Roddy Llewellyn, the well-known landscape gardener. Hang on though, I'd better explain why I decided on this series in the first place.

I am the owner of an extremely ramshackle cottage garden down in leafy Killinghurst where the grass in summer grows six feet tall and the nettles strain to outdo the brambles on the western marches. I like it that way, but the neighbours do not. They sometimes stop to inquire when I'm going to cut my grass, because any time now the judges for the prettiest village in England competition will be coming. My erstwhile neighbour Marigold once cut the lawn for me, which was kind. What makes things worse is that my new neighbour at Pillar Box Cottage has the tidiest garden you ever saw. Not a crocus out of place, the lawn like an acre of green linoleum, and even the rustic fence looking as if it's given a once-over with Mr Sheen on Sundays. I greatly admire it and stand in awe at all this dusting and polishing but I secretly like my own garden. I like the idea of my house looking as if it's standing in the middle of a field as opposed to the middle of New Malden.

The other morning I heard a programme about gardening on the wireless. Richard Baker was asking Candida Lycett Green, the horticultural expert, whether you could tell people's characters from their gardens. 'Certainly,' said Ms LG, who appeared to be accommodating several pounds of plums in her mouth.

'Well let's try you out,' said Mr B. 'What if you saw a

garden which had nettles everywhere, weeds on the paths, weeds in the beds, flowers growing higgledy-piggledy, dandelions and daisies on the lawn. What would the owners be like?'

'We-e-e-ll,' said Ms LG guardedly, 'I'd say they were rather untidy people who probably baked their own bread.'

'Very interesting indeed,' said Mr B. 'Let's try another. Suppose the garden was terribly tidy, not a daisy in sight, the edges trimmed the hedges clipped. What then?'

'Oh, that's easy,' said Ms LG (I said she was an expert). 'The owners are jolly tidy, organised people.'

Oh, if only, I thought, tipping tea leaves on to my cotoneaster – or was it my winter-flowering jasmine? – if only I knew as much about gardens, or indeed about human nature, as Ms Candida Lycett Green.

Without further preamble, let us plunge straight into the celebrity interview. This week, regardless of expense – well £18 actually, the cost of a return ticket from Hammersmith to leafy Killinghurst – I give you Mr Roddy Llewellyn. He, you may recall, achieved a certain notoriety back in the Seventies for his hot-house activities in Mustique with HRH Princess Margaret, but is now more preoccupied with grassroots issues, especially allotments, as gardening correspondent for the *Daily Star*.

Mr Llewellyn's business card says 'Roddy Llewellyn Landscapes' down one side in green squiggly writing, which sounds as if he's into palettes and smocks, but all is revealed in the small print at the bottom right-hand corner – 'Design and Contract Management for Town and Country Gardens'. It is not a business card so much as a piece of paper folded in half. When you open it there is a rather fine line-drawing of the top half of the owner, also in green, so that when I collected him at the station to drive him to my jungle clearing I had no difficulty recognising him.

Roddy Llewellyn learnt the nuts and bolts of his profession at Merrist Wood near Guildford, an academy famous for its diplomas in everything to do with horticulture, from estate management to pot plants. The only other person I know who went there was a hypermacho fellow called Dave who took a course in arboriculture and was last seen heading for British Columbia with an axe over his shoulder, a red-spotted kerchief tied to the shaft.

Mr Llewellyn, I was relieved to discover, is an altogether different species. He was wearing impeccable cavalry twills, a bespoke tweed jacket, and glasses like Ludovic Kennedy, in short every inch the society landscape gardener. To mention him in the same breath as Bill Sowerbutts is to compare Mustique with Morecambe. He *exudes* refinement. Here is a man, you feel, who knows instinctively what is *right*, a man who has mixed with people who have shrubberies and orchid houses and gazebos and terraces without a single item from Peter Jones's garden department. Three hundred years ago Louis XIV would have asked Roddy Llewellyn to help him plan his little patch out at Versailles.

I drove him carefully to Killinghurst – he has recently lost his driving licence and would greatly appreciate offers of work adjacent to the Number 11 bus route. We passed a man setting up his camera to take a picture of a clump of primroses. When he had taken it, the man slung his camera over his shoulder, trampled over the primroses and got back into his car. Mr Llewellyn sighed.

What sort of things does he write about in the *Star*? That morning, he said, he had had his usual heavy mailbag – a letter from a reader saying she had shocking bronchitis and wondered what kind of house-plants he would advise? Another woman wrote from Edgbaston to say she had just buried her late husband's ashes in the rockery and what should she grow on top?

It was when young Roddy, aged three, was given his first

tulip bulb to plant that his interest in all things green and beautiful began. His family's home in Wales, overlooking the Sugar Loaf, the Black Mountains and the sea, is a natural garden but his particular interest was cacti.

There is a horticultural tradition in the family. His great-grandfather introduced the bamboo to these islands, his uncle owns Shrublands in Suffolk, now a health farm but still famous for its gracious landscaping, and his father, Colonel Harry Llewellyn, equestrian extraordinary with a string of successful showjumpers in his stables, no doubt supplied the fertiliser.

While I made tea, Mr Llewellyn spent an hour wandering over my rubble, chicken wire and nettle culture. When he returned he was charming but businesslike. 'It's all delightfully shambolic,' he said, 'we mustn't spoil the – er – natural effect but I do think a little terracing would help. Get rid of that awful Leylandii hedge, clear the ground under the apple tree and plant, let me see, *Symphoricarpos chenaultii* "Hancock" as ground cover, no, no – on second thoughts, lay down a few branches and plant three *Clematis montana* and you'll get a wonderful cushiony effect. You need a Kiftsgate climbing rose against that telegraph pole, and by the way your camellia is distinctly chlorotic etc, etc.'

I was delighted, but who would undertake these earthworks? Mr Llewellyn bowed. 'Me,' he said. I looked at his fingernails which had perfect half-moons round the cuticles. 'I learnt all that practical stuff at Merrist Wood,' he said.

What should be avoided in a garden? Mr Llewellyn drew up a list of nasties: straight lines of red salvias, alternate planting of blue lobelia and white alyssum, *Prunus cerasifera* 'Pissardii' and Leylandii hedges.

What about gnomes? 'They're fine as long as they're peeping through something – that's recherché kitsch.'

Which reminds me – my second special offer, a ready-grown hedge of twenty-two seven-foot tall, exceedingly vigorous Leylandii conifers. They are yours for a fiver if you dig them up yourself, or in part-exchange for a box of *Symphoricarpos chenaultii* 'Hancock'. Now I can't say fairer than that.

With Mr Llewellyn's advice ringing in my ears, I set off for Crowthers, the garden statue emporium, to pick up a small Greek temple (nothing too ostentatious, a plain-ish nine-foot diameter Corinthian pillar job) for the west lawn. On the bus I thumbed through the current issue of the *Smithsonian* magazine. Do you know the *Smithsonian*? You should. It's a wonderfully fat, glossy, erudite American publication full of academic articles about heraldry and pithos pots and the history of flight, so I had a quick flick through it. And there it was: a full page advertisement showing a hand sprinkling something out of a small green tin with the caption, '*All you need for your garden is a can opener.*'

That's funny, I thought. Roddy Llewellyn didn't say anything about tin openers. I read the small print. In this one small can, indicated the ad, there is enough wildflower seed to turn your back garden into a meadow – an explosion of colour. From early spring to late autumn, Meadow in a Can will provide a carpet of blooms changing from the pale yellows of spring, the vivid scarlets and brilliant sapphires of summer to the copper and gold of autumn. Minimum maintenance, just mow it once a year, and all for a mere $20 or, if you wanted a big meadow, take the bumper 40-can pack and have yourself an acre of meadow for just $750 (£500 or so).

You see my problem, in a word – identity. Years ago I shared a flat with, among others, a deeply serious young financial journalist called Hamish who got married to another deeply serious young financial journalist called Frances and they seemed to be taking the devil of a long time finding a house in which to pursue their marital bliss.

'What's the problem Hamish?' I asked. 'There must be hundreds of houses for sale.'

'Oh there are, there are,' said Hamish gloomily, 'but it's a question of identity. I mean *is* one a Victorian villa in Putney or *is* one an Edwardian terrace in Kentish Town, or then again *is* one a maisonette in Notting Hill?'

For the record, it transpired that Hamish and Frances were Canonbury Georgian with Habitat overtones, but I now appreciate their difficulty. Was my modest patch in leafy Killinghurst a miniature Hampton Court, a Mrs Tiggy-winkle country garden with lavender bushes, a Keats Ode full of heady scents and heavy-headed peonies, or a Smithsonian meadow?

Only one way to find out. I telephoned my favourite BBC horticultural agony uncle, Alan Titchmarsh. Of all the media gardening pundits – the garrulous Geoffrey Smith, the academic Professor Gemmell, and the unpronounceable Stephan Buczacki – Mr Titchmarsh is the most infectious. He's so enthusiastic. Lying in bed on Saturday mornings I listen to Mr Titchmarsh bouncing round Wisley, tossing out advice on paraquat and mulch, and I feel moved to rush out, grab a spade, dig a large round flower bed and plant it full of pink and purple tulips that will grow into the shape of a clock. Trouble is, I can never find the spade.

Mr Titchmarsh rallied to the emergency. He came hot foot from his home in Alton, leapt out of his white Volvo estate, pausing only to smooth his rugger shirt over his lithe frame before he was off, running lightly across my dandelions and daisies, issuing instructions and Latinate names like a dragon blowing smoke.

So much for temples. 'What you've got here,' said Mr Titchmarsh, 'is a corner of a wood, an ancient wood, possibly medieval – you can tell by the dog's mercury – so you should leave it that way. Keep it wild. Chibble away a bit of grass here and there, sow a couple of packets of Woolworth's wildflower seeds – moon daisies, corncockles, larkspur, melilots, cornflowers, wild scabious (you've already got daisies and dandelions), and they'll grow up through the grass. Don't fret about the Leylandii hedge; it's only snobbery that makes it unfashionable. Trim it well back and it's as good as yew. Grow ivy up that bare wall (wire it first) – "Brokamp", which turns maroon in winter, "Goldheart" and plain dark green "Cristata" with frilly leaves. *Clematis tangutica*, fancy green leaves, little yellow lanterns and silky pompoms, you'll love that. Climbing roses of course, everyone has "Kiftsgate", why don't you try "La Mortola", pale grey leaves, white flowers; or even "Brenda Colvin" or *Rosa banksiae* "Lutea"?

'The nettles? Why cut down the nettles? Don't you like butterflies, tortoise-shell, peacock, admirals? They eat nettles. And why not have a herb garden? This is a marvellous spot.'

'But it *is* a herb garden,' I said. 'Look, here's rosemary, chives, thyme, sage . . .'

'That's not rosemary, that's cotton lavender and that "sage" is cistus. I say, you haven't been putting it in your soup, have you?'

'Yes,' I said, 'I have. And sauces and stews. It's particularly good with fish.'

The light was fading fast when we retired to the fireside. Mr Titchmarsh said that gardening journalism was a bit stereotyped and '*Now is the time of year to . . .*' He would like to take a more sideways look at the subject.

Rather like the sideways look I'm having to take at my temple. I particularly fancied the seventeenth-century Istrian marble one with the wrought-iron dome and Ionic columns with seating between – a mere £20,000 excluding fountain and statuary. Still, if I can get away with a couple of packets of Woolworth's seeds . . .

The proof of the puddynge

I had an invitation from the Hon. Mrs Grania Fitzherbert to attend one of her advanced cooking demonstrations at her Elizabethan manor house in Wiltshire. Chokely Manor, said the invitation, was a magnificent period house much frequented in its heyday by the Cecils, Seymours and Howards, and Queen Elizabeth had almost certainly slept in the West Wing. To mark the first of Mrs Fitzherbert's one-day courses, she had chosen a period theme – The Tudor Table – and a typical sixteenth-century lunch was included in the 25 guinea fee. Now while I have no particular yen to cook turnips with brawn in ramekins or Master Taplow's pigeons in parchment and least of all lark's eggs in aspic, the prospect of a day out of London outweighed this niggling consideration and I set out for Paddington with a light step.

The countryside round Chokely was scrubby and flat and the unspoilt village in which it lay had double yellow lines in the high street and a one-way filter system round the village green. The manor was impressive, though little of the original survived. Beneath the West Wing where the Faerie Queen may or may not have brushed her teeth, there now stood a large double garage housing a silver Bentley and a Volvo Estate. I tugged at the bell rope and a clarion peal worthy of Westminster Cathedral echoed within. The door was opened by an ageing family retainer, or at any rate a grey-haired chap in cavalry twills who handed me a goblet of something hot and rust-coloured with tadpoles or tea leaves floating on top. 'What is it?' I asked.

'A posset,' he replied doubtfully and led me through to an anteroom where the other neo-Elizabethans were already assembled.

There were eight of us – three wives from the nearby American airbase, Nancy, Jo-Anne and Charleen, dressed for a society wedding in crisp linen suits; two Sloane Rangers, Camilla and Sophie, who were thinking of going into catering; a nervous girl called Lucy who said she was getting married next month and didn't know how to boil an egg let alone a lark's egg in aspic; and a strange little man in red jacket and blue trousers, like Noddy except that he was Hungarian.

'Are you interested in Tudor food?' I asked him.

'Excuse me,' he said.

'What is your special interest, the food or the history?' I said.

'Thank you I am sufficient,' he replied, clicking his heels together.

Further conversation was forestalled by the arrival of our hostess, Mrs Fitzherbert, who was tall and dreamy and wearing a pink dress with leg-of-mutton sleeves and a ruff, like pictures I've seen of the young Elizabeth Tudor in the gardens of Kenilworth.

'Do come through and bring your possets,' she said and led us to a large flagstoned kitchen with oak beams and copper pans big enough to boil whole swans, hogs, cawls and several weeks' worth of porridge for Cecils, Howards, Seymours and even Fitzherberts. There was a counter dividing the kitchen in two, made of Formica-coated wattle and daub, on which stood a welter of gadgets, mixers, juicers, slicers etc. We sat on benches on one side and Mrs F. put on a frilly apron and began demonstrating.

It was all very interesting at the time though I've quite forgotten how to do it now. The biggest problem seems to be getting your hands on Elizabethan produce. While at a pinch a Tesco's frozen duckling can substitute for a swan, I'm not so sure that a Wall's collar of gammon would make such a tasty hedgehog broth as Mistress Quickly might have made.

As she worked Mrs Fitzherbert prattled merrily about life in Tudor England. She told us about Sir Walter Raleigh and the Spanish Armada and Sir Philip Sidney and William Shakespeare, who she said wrote some very great plays. Nancy from the airbase asked at what stage the hedgehog broth could be frozen. Halfway through dishing up her Poor Knights of Windsor Puddynge Mrs F. gave a dramatic reconstruction of the trial of Mary Queen of Scots, playing the parts of both Queens herself. The bride-to-be asked which way up you stood watercress to keep it fresh. Camilla and Sophie took three reels of film of the roast swan.

We had lunch in the Great Hall where the ageing family retainer turned out to be Freddie Fitzherbert, Master of Chokely, who handled the wines. Freddie had obviously handled a lot of wine that morning for his nose was flushed and he asked me three times, as he passed me the capon in cider, if I'd care for a slice of cake.

After lunch we walked round the delightful knot garden and Charleen said it was all so very very gracious. I asked Sophie what sort of catering she wanted to go into. Films and telly, she said, there was so much historic drama nowadays that someone needed to know about Raj banquets, Roman orgies, and what Vasco da Gama ate as he filled in his log.

I'm thinking of starting one-day courses myself to earn a little pin money. My first is called Six Centuries of Prison Fare and I shall wear a ball and chain as I cook. The 25 guinea fee will include a fascinating variety of different breads and gruels made from potato peels, husks and scraps, and I have already got hold of eight different types of water, though naturally my husband handles this side of things. My biggest problem is getting hold of weevils, and I'd be grateful if anyone could suggest a reliable supplier . . .

You Tarzan, me Sue

It all started at Floors Castle last October. I had gone up to
Scotland to interview that most gracious of young couples,
the Duke and Duchess of Roxburghe, in their magnificent
family home, and on our way up to the nursery for high tea –
Lady Rose, four, the Marquis of Bowmont and Cessford,
two, Nanny Robertson and I – the Duchess happened to
mention that His Grace would not be joining us because he
was busy talking to the people from Warner Brothers outside.

Warner Brothers? Somehow amid all the stately bric-à-
brac, the suits of armour, tapestries and glass cases, the
mention of Warner Brothers seemed faintly irreverent, like
belching in church. What on earth was the tenth Duke up to?
Renting out his ancestral seat for another Tarzan film or
something?

Well yes, as a matter of fact, that is precisely what His
Grace was doing.

'I must say I am surprised at you, Your Grace,' I said to the
Duchess. 'I know times are hard and I dare say running a
castle comes expensive, what with all those birds to re-stuff
and turrets to re-crenellate, but isn't letting off your ban-
queting hall to Charles Atlas and a load of gorillas pushing it a
bit?'

The Duchess explained mildly that this was not the usual
macho monkey affair beloved of cheapskate film-makers
since 1918. This was, in fact, a rather intellectual version of
the book, with Sir Ralph Richardson playing the hero's

grandfather. Besides, it was being directed by the chap who directed *Chariots of Fire* – what was his name again – Hugh Hefner, that was it.

'Hugh *Hudson*, Your Grace,' murmured Nanny, pouring milk into the Marquis of Bowmont and Cessford's Peter Rabbit mug.

'Oh that's it, Hudson, charming man,' said Her Grace. 'No, Rosie, bread and butter before cake. Well anyway, they've been here all day marching about and measuring things. I know, why don't we ask them to give you a lift back to Edinburgh airport?'

And that, dear reader, is how I came to meet the charming Mr Hudson, who told me at length and with earnestness exactly how different his film *Greystoke* was going to be from its forty-three predecessors, and for that matter how different it was going to be from any other film, period. It was a story about choices, about conflicting moralities, about the meaning of civilisation and the nature of freedom. I have never met a film director before, and if they are all as charming as Mr Hudson I have clearly been missing out.

In the fullness of time I had a Christmas card from Greystoke Productions inviting me down to Elstree, and at 11.15 last Tuesday a limo arrived to take me there.

'Here we are,' said Miss Darcy, the publicity lady, opening the door of an oversize hangar. 'Be careful because it is a bit wet underfoot,' and we walked slap into an equatorial jungle. There were forty-foot philodendrons, thirty-foot dracaena, acres of bamboo, bromeliads and coffee plants, muddy paths overhung with creeper, strange monsteras swaying in the branches and, after we had pushed our way through half a mile of undergrowth, a murky lagoon in which an ape was floating on its back.

'What is the ape doing?' I asked Miss Darcy, for want of anything better to say. What *can* you say about a piece of genuine African jungle six miles from Watford?

'I think it's dead,' said Miss Darcy, referring to her script with a worried expression. 'Can't apes swim?'

'No they can't,' said a voice behind us, 'they don't have sufficient adipose tissue to keep them afloat.'

'May I introduce Professor Fouts of Oklahoma University, our resident primatology consultant,' said Miss Darcy.

We paddled back to the main filming area. High above our heads Mr Hudson could be seen inside a crane with a polythene sheet over his head. Everyone on the set was wearing anoraks, gumboots and sou'westers, and I was about to ask Miss Darcy why when someone shouted 'Start the rain!' and several thousand gallons of water drenched the studio. Through the torrent I could just make out a pair of apes chasing each other through the tree trunks.

'OK, break for lunch,' shouted the rainmaker, and Mr Hudson descended from his aerial perch in the manner of Moses coming down from the mountain.

'We'll grab a word if we can,' whispered Miss Darcy, 'but because he is the producer as well as the director he has so many things to attend to.

'*Greystoke* is the biggest film being made anywhere in the world at the moment.' (Its budget is $17 million.)

Various supplicants were besieging Mr Hudson with bits of paper. Wearily he authorised the purchase of another 600 philodendrons, twelve more apes, hotel bookings for the unit in the Cameroons. 'What's this for?' he asked a man proffering a rather smaller piece of officialdom.

'It's the lunch menu, Mr Hudson, sir, would you like grilled pork chop or lemon sole?'

Too bad there isn't room to tell you about Tarzan, who is pale and French and cerebral, or the tiger cub or what Princess Anne said to one of the apes. Tell you what – nearer its release I'll do what they call a Major Colour Piece about *Greystoke* – unless of course Visconti has decided to make another version.

Toots and saddles

Don't laugh. I've just been to a hunt ball. It was, I hasten to say, my friend Melissa's idea. I personally loathe the sport, not because of the cruel hunters (who actually look rather sexy in those Peter Jones table-mat outfits) or even because of the poor little fox. I reckon a canny fox can look after itself. A soft-hearted neighbour once told me in confidence that one hunting day a breathless and pretty washed-up looking fox came tearing into her garden, the pack in full cry not 200 yards behind. Quick as a flash she opened the back door and offered refuge in the spare bedroom, whence they both looked out of the window at the puzzled hunters poking about in her dahlias.

No, it isn't poor little Reynard, it's poor little Beulah my hypersensitive Siamese cat that I worry about. Whenever the hunt meets outside our house she has a breakdown. When we first moved to our centuries-old, tile-hung, roses-round-the-door cottage and learned that the hunt often foregathered on the road outside, I was enchanted. I saw myself winsomely clad in dimity homespun running merrily out of the aforesaid rose-encrusted door to greet the colourful scene, a foaming stirrup cup (whatever that is) in my hands, crying a greeting on the lines of, 'Good morrow to you, gentlemen. Prithee wet your whistles on this cup brewed by my own hands this Lammastide.'

'Why, 'tis Mistress Arnold herself,' returns Sir Richard, slapping his thigh, leaning down from his saddle and lifting me aloft – a complicated manoeuvre but huntsmen are no fools – 'a thousand thanks and may you be the mother of many strong-limbed whippers-in.' Or words to that effect.

Sadly, this is not the case. So far I have not developed what you could honestly call a slap-and-stirrup-cup relationship with our Master of Fox Hounds. I was recently ordered off a corner of his 600 acres by an unsmiling gamekeeper who accused me of wilful trespass as I strolled carelessly along a cart-track carpeted with bluebells and primroses. 'But I was only admiring the pretty flowers,' I said as he escorted me off the land. Some days later I received a curt note from the MFH saying that arboreal strolls were strictly forbidden. *Enfin*. No strolls, no stirrup cup.

So what was quisling Arnold doing, you ask, at a hunt ball? Well, Melissa's father, who is handsome and debonair and a pal of Mrs Thatcher and something unbelievably big in the City, has just been promoted to MFH. I think he rides as well. The most unlikely folk are taking to the saddle these days, starting with Victor Lowndes, the ex-Playboy director, who's crazy about the sport. He doesn't fall off as much as he used to, either.

Won't it be the original thrash, I said doubtfully, full of the original thrashing bores?

Melissa said it was time I saw how the other half lived and would I please stop talking ignorantly about twenty-five dogs barking in the woods when I actually meant twelve and a half couple of hound speaking in the covers.

The event was held in a huge concrete building like a circus tent. I understand it was a country club; it could easily accommodate next year's Commonwealth Games. I sat next to two extremely young, extremely clean-shaven Army officers. The one on my left said living in Pirbright was jolly good fun, and if I didn't want the rest of my breaded pork chop and sauté potatoes could he have it? The one on my right said a short-service commission got you just as far as a degree. He had just landed a job in an up-market estate agents.

I performed an enthusiastic foxtrot round the athletics track with yet another Sandhurst alumnus who said without malice, 'My God, I wish I'd met you ten years ago,' and I was beginning to feel just a little bit depressed when the Master himself, resplendent in white tie and pink tails, offered to introduce me to the huntsmen, i.e. the professional hunt officers, who were sitting by themselves at a table outside the ballroom. We were joined by various décolletée fillies and a splendid fellow in moss green tails, designed by himself. His wife was the outgoing MFH, he said gloomily, and bought us all champagne to celebrate her retirement. There followed a heated debate as to which of the three sports was the most exciting – the tickle of a salmon on the end of the line, the thrill of a bird on the end of a gun or the incomparable beauty of the View Halloo when the fox has been cornered.

I found all this talk of mutilation and murder a trifle discouraging and sought to change the subject by offering round some free samples of 'Jules', the new fragrance for men from Christian Dior. Who knows, it might put the hounds off the scent?

Melissa arrived a little flushed. 'Come on, let's go to the lav for a quick toot,' she said. Another of those hunting terms, I dare say.

Rock bottom

'But what is the point,' I asked, 'of my learning how to operate a one-man submarine?'

I am as eager as anyone to spring into pastures new and am even now negotiating a package deal to Poona so that I, too, may sit at the feet of the Bhagwan Shree Rajneesh and find true happiness; but submarines have not so far played a dominant role in my life.

'You could wander through the most beautiful kelp forests on the sea bed and inspect ancient wrecks,' said the young man from the submarine school.

'I wouldn't know a kelp, beautiful or otherwise, if I bumped into one,' I said. 'And as for inspecting ancient wrecks, I have this mirror in the bathroom . . .'

The young man was persuasive and I am easily persuaded. He told me tales of Spanish gold buried in creaking galleons at the bottom of the ocean, of floating weightlessly over underwater cliffs encrusted with sea-roses, of being chased by killer whales through Norwegian fjords, and of watching shoals of iridescent fish with tails like stained-glass windows amid the coral of the Great Barrier Reef.

'You're on,' I said. 'Take me to your submarine.'

It was yellow, of course, bright yellow, and the size and shape of a motorcycle sidecar. I was glad he had mentioned kelp and the iridescent fish first because it was hard to think romantically about the car-park of Brighton Marina, where the sub was moored. A Mars Bar wrapper and two cigarette butts floated by in the brackish water on the way to Dieppe.

'Come on,' said the young man, handing me a boiler suit. 'I'll put you through the basic training.'

First let me blind you with a little science. The submarine was, in fact, a submersible called a K350. It costs around £20,000 to the man who's got everything including a yacht to haul it around, weighs 1½ tons and runs on batteries. With three thruster motors, one at each side and one at the back, it can proceed along the seabed at four knots.

OK, said the young man, time to climb in. He opened a round lid like a dustbin's on top of the vessel and guided me in. He then painstakingly explained the complicated collection of instruments, knobs, handles, valves, nuts, bolts, levers, wires, leads, buttons and bows that lined the metal walls. There were portholes just underneath the dustbin lid and a large one in the front at ankle level. There were, I was relieved to hear, any number of safety devices in the way of extra oxygen supplies that would last for four days, not to mention emergency exits. There were also things called scrubbers for getting rid of the carbon monoxide and a rather unpleasant affair called an oral nasal through which you could breathe surface oxygen.

'Fine,' said the young man. 'Time you took a dive.'

'Are you sure I'm ready?' I asked, feeling the panic begin to rise. 'I don't think I've quite got the hang of it.'

'You'll be fine,' he said. 'We'll be in communication with you throughout, here's the check list. Down you go.'

'Look,' I said, 'I know it's officially a one-man sub but I'm amazingly small and light and adaptable, so would it be against the rules of the Cinque Ports for you to come down with me?'

The young man consulted with his business partner, a charming Welshman called Joe who had had to retire from deep-sea diving after a heart operation. Joe now has two plastic valves which tick noisily under his sweater. 'You could ditch those two 40lb lead weights, I suppose, and take her on instead,' said Joe.

They ditched the weights. I crouched in between the two small wheels that operated the port and starboard motors, and the young man squatted behind me, his knees either side of my shoulders. We battened down the hatch. 'Sub to surface,' said the young man into the mike. 'Venting now. Over.'

Slowly, gently with odd gurgling sounds coming from all sides like umpteen plugs being pulled out of umpteen bathtubs, we began to sink. It was a most satisfying feeling. I was tempted to shout 'Up periscope!' like Jack Hawkins in one of those naval epics. But only fighting submarines had periscopes, said the young man. There was a bump as we hit the bottom. The depth gauge was showing fifteen feet, which counts for ocean bottom in Brighton Marina. I scoured the water beyond the forward porthole for a smidgeon of coral, a hint of a kelp. The Mars Bar wrapper floated silently past.

Ah well. If ever I do find myself surrounded by doubloons amongst the coral of the Barrier Reef, at least I'll know how to operate my thrusters correctly.

The tartan trail

About six doors down from a rather fine cheese shop at Comrie, in Tayside, where I bought half a pound of mature Aberdeen cheddar and enough oatcake to see me through the winter, I chanced upon an inviting doorway, dark and low and bearing the title The Museum of Scottish Tartans. I am not a museum enthusiast. I like flamboyant exhibitions such as Dr Roy Strong is wont to stage every so often. But I find it hard to marvel at serried ranks of military medals under acres of glass like forced tomatoes, or a pair of rusty rowlocks purporting to come from the boathouse of Shalott. I suppose it's because I never got further than 1603 in history and would far rather sit on a bench *outside* the museum, reading the local rag.

However, there were two good reasons to visit this one – a sudden downpour and the fact that my maiden name is McHarg. Since I am fast approaching the sere and yellow leaf of my life, when I shall need a tartan rug to tuck about my knees in the car, I thought I might as well get the tartan to which I am congenitally entitled.

This is not the first time I have tried to root out the tartan truffles of the Clan McHarg. Years ago in Edinburgh I was seduced into one of the many 'find your own tartan' shops. After thumbing in a desultory fashion through a couple of leaflets, the resident tartanologist told me that the McHargs were not Scottish at all but mere Irish bog-trotters who had come over steerage on the Stranraer ferry circa 1900. They certainly did not have a tartan, he said. He implied that they did not have shoes either.

I told this sorry tale to Dr Micheil MacDonald, curator of The Tartans Museum. He listened attentively, stroking his bushy black chin, and said, 'Nonsense, the McHargs were as Scottish as spurtles,' and if I would accompany him to the research department upstairs he would tell me all.

If ever I needed to lay a few acres waste with fire and the sword, I should call upon Dr MacDonald to assist. He is a splendid figure of a man, tall, bulky, bearded, rugged, lofty of brow, lengthy of leg, the 100-year-old kilt he always wears sitting squarely on his paunch, and slung about at the waist with a leather money-pouch. Those itchy-looking sporrans are a relatively modern invention. I followed him up the wooden stairs, musing inconsequentially that there is nothing that shows off a fine masculine physique like a kilt. Dr MacD in trousers would have been as unthinkable as the Colossus in drag.

But I am getting carried away. We were talking of tartan. First thing Dr MacD does is to look up the Houston, Texas, telephone directory, where, he says, you will find almost every Scottish name there is. There is a MacFark and a McHorse but no McHarg. He pulls down another tome of the size of the Book of Kells and riffles through it. 'Here we are, MacHans, MacHardie, MacHarg . . . fifteenth-century name, prevalent in Carrick and the mountainous parts of Galloway, common today in Glasgow, also spelt M'Quarg. 1581 Finlay M'Quharge charged with fire-raising and burning of houses belonging to Stewart of Fintillauch. 1684 Margaret Machharge charged with being a disorderly person in the parish of Cross-Michael. Also Jean M'Harg in Troquhan in 1713 . . .'

'OK, I get the drift,' I said. 'What about my tartan?'

Dr MacDonald fished about in a chest of drawers and pulled out a small square of cloth in various muted shades of lovat, moss, sage and conifer, with a white horizontal and an orange vertical stripe – very pretty but hardly fire-raising garb.

So much for the McHargs. The museum itself is a gem and justifiably won the Best Small Museum Award a couple of years back. It is crammed with unfusty information, ancient order books, 1,300 tartans, cartoons, dotty records (the longest Scottish surname is MacGhillisheathanaich; the shortest is Og), a piece of MacBean tartan taken to the moon by astronaut Alan Bean.

I was lucky to find the good Doctor, an anthropologist by profession, for he is often abroad staging hugely successful exhibitions. At a recent trade fair in Tokyo, The Tartans Museum stand, depicting the uncanny similarities between the clansmen and the samurai, stole the show. And all this on a shoe-string budget. What Dr MacDonald gets to run the place doesn't even pay for a full-time secretary.

Come on you fifty million souls around the world with Scots blood coursing through your veins. Dinna be careful. Bring forrit the tartan. Dig deep into your sporrans and support your heritage. Cheques payable to MacDonald or even McHarg. I promise to pass them on.

Opening claws

First let me tell you about the lobster. My God! What a lobster! Never have I seen such a lobster. It was a Titan, a Colossus, a Leviathan, a *corker* of a lobster, a veritable Behemoth of swollen flesh encased in dimpled, wrinkled, crumpled black armour. There it squatted on the wooden planks of Oban pier, massy, meaty, Goliath turned crustacean, a megalith of clammy corpulence daring you to think of mayonnaise and maybe a small green salad on the side.

We bought it. The fishwife said it was the last and the least of the four that had come in that morning, weighing a mere 4½ pounds. We carried it home on a gilded litter – well, we would have, but a blue plastic bucket was handier. It didn't (as I feared it might) scream when cast into the furnace – did Samson scream, did Hercules whimper? – but bore its fate with the stoical dignity that befits a fallen giant. We split it down the middle, called for dressing and abandoned ourselves to the sins of the flesh. Bramble the cat went berserk in anticipation, rubbing its back frenziedly against our legs, pleading for a taste. It was indeed a moment of peculiar splendour such as is offered only once or twice in a lifetime.

I don't actually like shellfish. I was once advised by my best friend, after we had lunched off crab in black bean sauce at a Chinese restaurant in Wardour Street, that if I seriously wanted to make friends and influence people I must *never* eat shellfish in public because I make such a filthy mess.

The Oban Experience has changed all that. Now I crave crab, pray for prawns, lust after langoustines. My lobster-sharing companion said that this was the only way to eat lobster – within hours of its being potted. 'Unless it's absolutely fresh, forget it,' he said, expertly cracking open a claw and extracting a gargantuan, rosy wodge of thigh. He should know because he was once in the business himself. He used to drive a load of live, wriggling langoustines once a week from Port Appin in Argyll non-stop to London for delivery to the better fish restaurants. The idea was to sell them before they collapsed and died from jet lag. Nobody loves a dead langoustine.

Some days later I found myself supperless late on a Sunday night in Knutsford, a pretty market town just outside Manchester. I made inquiries and was directed to the Chinese restaurant in the main drag. It had the seating capacity of a Mecca ballroom but there were only two other diners. First thing I see on the menu is lobster and, misty with nostalgia, I order sweet and sour lobster, deep fried lobster balls, lobster pancakes and lobster chow mien. My companion settles for four other dishes, we're pretty peckish, and we summon the waiter. He is a tall youth with sleepy eyes and an insolent manner who writes down our eight dishes in his order book and then says, 'What about a main course?'

We are surprised. We had not realised that our eight dishes (all costing around £2 a shot), are only starters. We say we do not want a main course, whereupon Sleepyeyes snaps shut his notebook and barks, 'You not allowed eat only starters. Must have main course. Rule of house.'

We are patient. We do quick sums on our paper napkins and point out that eight starters cost near enough £20 whereas two main dishes – a modest chop suey, say, and beef in special sunflower sauce – would come to a mere £6.60. Sleepyeyes is adamant. 'No main course no dinner,' he repeats. 'Management rule.'

Listen, we say, prepared to be helpful because it is Sunday night in Knutsford and loaves and fishes, let alone sweet and sour lobster, are thin on the ground. 'We don't want a main course but we'll buy *you* a main course. What would you like to eat while we eat our eight first courses?'

The youth retires muttering and returns with a tall, beautiful, unsmiling Chinese lady who it turns out is *in loco patronis*. We explain the situation, show her the financial logic of our defence, and offer to buy her a main course too. She is unmoved. 'No starters without main course,' she says. 'No main course no meal. It is the rule.'

We leave. No taxation without representation, no friendly service and management cooperation, no dice. It is the principle. I was sad about the robster, sorry *lobster*. I'm sure it would have been excellent. I understand Sleepyeyes gets up at crack of dawn every morning to buy them dripping fresh from Knutsford pier.

It is time to talk turkey again. It is time to ponder, as I do every year, whether the traditional Christmas bird is not a tedious and tiresome commodity, to be seasoned and stuffed and stitched and trussed and basted and tested and heaved in and out of the oven with breaking back and sweating brow and sinking heart; for in my long experience, no matter how you cosset and care for the brute, no matter how you robe it with voluptuous bacon brassières and serve it garnished like an over-dressed dowager with watercress and chipolatas, the result is always the same – a pale plank of reconstituted chipboard in the name of breast, or a wodge of oaken sinew hewn from one gargantuan thigh. Is it really worth it?

Only once in my life have I tasted a turkey that made me lick my lips and call for more. That was in Dublin at the home of a very dear friend. It was Boxing Day as I recall and, resigned to the inevitable spread of cold sawdust with Cumberland sauce, I was astounded at the succulent, tangy morsels of cold roast fowl that she heaped upon my plate. What was the secret?

Well, she said, it was a home grown bird, slaughtered ten days before Christmas by the local farmer, left to hang in his shed like a pheasant for a week and then stuffed with a couple of pounds of rough old beef shin or maybe shank. Thereafter it was cooked at a spanking pace in a turf-fired oven, the beef moistening and flavouring the meat in the process.

I should perhaps mention that it was the same friend who sent her cousin in England a turkey one Christmas.

Delighted, the cousin loaded it straight into the oven on Christmas morning. Scarcely had the family returned from church, their appetites pleasantly whetted by the aromas exuding from the kitchen, when there was a great explosion within. The door of the oven had blown off, the turkey lay in tatters and buried deep within the nether cavity were the splintered remains of a bottle of poteen, secreted there to foil Her Majesty's Customs and Excise.

But tradition dies hard at Schloss Arnold, and I was gloomily resigning myself to the annual turkey drag when someone told me of an extraordinary phenomenon known as the self-basting turkey. Be warned, said my source, there are many self-basting birds on the market but only one, the Golden Norfolk, bastes with real dairy butter. A curious picture loomed before me of a semi-comatose bird soaking in my roasting tin like a weary wing-forward in the bath after a match, occasionally lifting an arm to dowse its limbs with the surrounding liquor.

Fool, said my source, they inject under its skin.

Good grief, I said, isn't that painful?

All of which preamble explains my presence recently at Great Witchingham in Norfolk, headquarters of Mr Bernard Matthews, the undisputed Napoleon of the turkey business. Mr Matthews produces more than five million turkeys every year for the table, half of which he sells as deep-frozen whole roasting birds, with or without the butter infusion. The rest he processes into deep-frozen turkey burgers, turkey sausages and a handy little number called the turkey roll. Mr Matthews started thirty years ago as an insurance clerk with twenty turkey eggs which he bought at an auction for £1. His business now has an annual turnover of £40 million – truly a tale of enterprise and dedication to warm the cockles of the deepest frozen hearts.

Alas for time and space to tell you the half of what I witnessed in Great Witchingham – the 30,000 eggs set every day in giant incubators, the day-old chicks travelling along conveyor belts like airline passengers on moving walkways, the deep litter houses full of turkey stags crying 'gobble gobble' in unison at visitors. And then the plant itself where every year 100,000 tons of turkey meat are processed by butchers wearing red and yellow crash-helmets, flinging spare parts into huge drums to be turned miraculously into twenty-foot lengths of deep frozen turkey roll like pink telegraph poles.

Afterwards Mr Matthews offered frankfurters made of turkey, streaky bacon made of turkey, smoked ham made of turkey and, the *pièce de resistance* for me, a whole cold roast turkey made entirely of boneless white meat which could be sliced like a loaf of bread. If my host had offered plum pudding and brandy butter made entirely from turkey feathers, I would not have been surprised.

I have just cooked my first Golden Norfolk self-basting turkey. Even as I write this I can hear it sizzling agreeably behind closed doors. It looks good, it smells good, and if the couple of pounds of rough old beef soaked in poteen that I carefully stuffed it with have worked their promised magic, I have no doubt that it will taste not unticklesome to the palate withal.

Foreign Parts

An Indian journal

'And how do you find Kashmir?' asked Mr Kumar politely, as we glided over the dark green grass of the Dal lake at Srinagar in sort of tented gondola called a *shikara*. Disconcertingly like Surrey, I wanted to say. No wonder homesick British colonials came flocking up here for their holidays. All those larch-lap fences skirting neat gardens, and prim little houses with attic dormers, could comfortably transfer to Camberley without raising a single Home Counties eyebrow. When the dying Mogul Emperor Jehangir was asked to name his last earthly desire, he opened his dimming eyes and whispered, 'Kashmir, only Kashmir.' I suppose 'Frimley, only Frimley,' hasn't quite the same ring.

Mr Kumar offered spiced Kashmiri tea, excellent, he said, for headaches, heartburn, influenza and dysentery. We sipped cinnamon tea. Somewhere a sitar moaned, peacocks strutted on the far shore and a faint whiff of incense wafted over the lapping water. So far so perfect. Three weeks of Indian delights lay ahead. We had letters of introduction to two maharajas and a brigadier, and to this end had packed crêpe-de-chine dresses and gold dancing sandals. The plan was to spend two days in Ladakh on the borders of Tibet visiting Buddhist monasteries on a quick Karma crawl, and then go back to Delhi and all those romantic places – Agra, Khajarho, Jaipur, Jaisalmer, Jodhpur . . . Mr Kumar blew his nose over the side of the boat.

'How long do you stay in Srinagar?' he asked. We said we had tickets to fly to Leh in the morning, and had even packed a cardigan apiece because Ladakh in early winter could be chilly at night. Mr Kumar looked surprised. There was no aeroplane to Leh in the morning, he said. The winter schedule had begun and the next flight was in five days, the very date we were due at the Lake Palace in Udaipur, maharajas and all.

So we went by bus. It was a B class bus. The A class bus only ran on Sundays. B stands for Basic Bus. It had four wheels and a ferocious fume-spewing engine and some-where, somehow, above the wheels and behind the engine, sat the passengers, goats, chickens, babies, sacks of rice, rolls of carpet and a flotilla of ever-burning kerosene stoves brewing up char. The journey to Leh takes two days with an overnight stop at a one-yak town called Kargil. The road crosses three majestic mountain passes, Zoji La, Fatu La and Namika La, all pushing 14,000 feet into thin air.

Did I say road? There is no road. There is a narrow ledge strewn with boulders and the corpses of lorries along which our Sikh driver plied his merry way at breakneck speed. There is no comforting barrier between the ledge and the edge, so that when I opened my eyes, just once (for the Srinagar Leh road is justifiably dubbed The Most Spectacu-lar Road on Earth), I could look straight down on to the wrecks of vehicles in the ravine 14,000 feet below.

We stopped at a military checkpoint. As this is a sensitive border area, the army controls the entire route. An officer peered in through the window. 'Only two overseas ladies,' he asked suspiciously. 'No gents accompanying?'

'No gents,' we whispered weakly.

The two unaccompanied ladies passed the night on the mud floor of the Dreamview Hotel at Kargil, a bucket being the 'attached bathroom', and on the morrow proceeded to Leh, taking in as many inaccessible monasteries perched high on crags or buried deep in gorges as their light summer footwear would allow. They tasted *tsampa*, the staple barley diet of the monks, drank tea laced with rancid yak butter, and heard lamas in strange yellow bonnets chanting mysterious chants. And at last they reached Leh airport on Monday morning for the 10 o'clock once-weekly flight to Delhi, for they had vowed that come hurricane or hellfire they would never *ever* travel the Most Spectacular Road on Earth again.

At 11 o'clock the booking clerk announced that due to engine failure the flight had been cancelled. When was the next one? Same time next week, he said. With heavy hearts the two unaccompanied ladies headed for a taxi to take them back across Namika La, Fatu La and Zoji La. That night they slept in a village called Drass, and early next morning it began to snow. By lunchtime fifteen feet of snow had fallen and four taxis, two B class buses, nine lorries, fifty army trucks, two unaccompanied ladies and a goat were stranded on the Most Spectacular Road on Earth somewhere in the Himalayas.

'It is no use,' said a soldier. 'The road is blocked both ways. You will sleep tonight in the trucks. It may take a week to clear the road. If it is not cleared by the 10th (it was now the 3rd) the road will officially close until the end of May. I am sorry.'

So were we. I was glad I'd brought my cardigan.

We divide into two groups. The eight elderly Americans from Ohio and their forty-three pieces of luggage are winched into the back of one truck, the rest of us clamber into another. It is 4 p.m., cold and getting colder, dark and getting darker and the snow keeps falling. My feet in dainty sandals are beginning to look and feel like raspberry ripple ice-cream, but rummaging in my bag I find two plastic carrier bags (thank God one is from Harrods) and put them over my tights and under the socks borrowed from Larry, a bearded anaesthesiologist from LA. I can now get out of the truck to pee without fear of frostbite.

Larry (who has seen a lot of those survival movies) speaks. 'OK you guys, we gotta make a plan. We gotta pool our resources. How many sleeping bags we got, how much food? And since we gonna be here some time, we better get acquainted.'

Huddled in a circle, knees covered with old sacks, backsides frozen on the wet, metal floor of the truck, we introduce ourselves. There's Larry and Maryanne from Laguna Beach, Dieter, a Lufthansa pilot and his blonde, giggly girlfriend. Bernard, an elderly French tax inspector, Pierre, a Belgian schoolteacher, Hervé de Monès Delibouix, a lanky Parisian student, Andrea, an Australian nurse, my companion Mrs P, Irish but living in St Anton, and one British ace reporter with a Harrods carrier on her left foot to prove it.

We pool the food, two biscuits, five walnuts and some cheese, not much if we're going to be here for a week. I feel sorry for the Australian nurse. It's always the nurse they eat first in those survival films. Three soldiers climb in with us and brew tea in a kerosene drum. They say the temperature drops to minus 20C at night. Larry gives us all sleeping pills called qualudes, which he says are all the rage in LA. They give you a buzz like cocaine before you drop off. We swallow our qualudes, start giggling maniacally and eventually fall asleep in a jumble of arms and legs.

The Lufthansa pilot leaves his size 11 feet in Mrs P's stomach all night. In the wee hours the soldier on my right attempts to share my sack in a less than platonic fashion. Should I protest at this shameless impropriety or be grateful for the extra body warmth? We compromise. At dawn we are woken by a strange dripping sound. Icicles are melting on to our heads. I crawl over thirteen bodies, lift up the flap and look out. Snow, snow, thick, thick snow. More landslides, two trucks are buried.

Mrs P and I empty the contents of our luggage and wear them. I am now lumpily clad in three pairs knickers, two prs tights, three T-shirts, a silk dress, dungarees, a cardigan, one pr carrier bags and a shirt wrapped round my head to shield my ears from the icy wind. A soldier returns with grim tidings. We shall not be moving over Zoji La pass to Srinagar for at least another three days. A peasant wrapped in a blanket and a goat across his shoulders passes. Where is he going? 'To Sonemarg, the village beyond Zoji La', he says, on foot. Hervé says he's going too. Mrs P and I opt to join them; we're still hoping to make the Lake Palace at Udaipur by Friday. The others are taking it in turns to squat under the truck.

Two kilometres on, the snow is up to my armpits and we give up. We are now at the front of the convoy and seek refuge in the front of a civilian lorry with two drivers and an Indian hitchhiker. At least it's warm. We drink tea and eat dal and the Sikh driver tells us his uncle went to London for an operation on his kidneys and came back in a box with his name on a brass plate. It was a very fine box, he says.

Night falls. The smell in the cab is pungent and I produce my bottle of Joy by way of room freshener. 'I love French perfume,' says the Sikh emptying £22 worth on to his turban. He rolls us all a joint. They too have run out of food. If we're to be hungry we might as well be high.

Another day, another night. Every morning the driver lights a kerosene stove under the fuel tank to defrost the diesel in case we can move on. On Thursday evening we are told the road will not be cleared and we must return to Drass, thirty kilometres back and, according to the records, the second coldest inhabited village in the world. The first is in Siberia.

Hervé, Mrs P and I are loaded into the back of a military truck carrying scrap iron. Five miles before Drass we hear a strange caterwauling. We peer out. Eight elderly Americans from Ohio are standing, sobbing, vomiting, praying by the roadside next to their forty-three pieces of luggage and a broken-down army truck. Can we give them a lift? We heave them in on top of the scrap iron, ripping fox-fur jackets, smashing Nikon cameras. It has started to snow again.

Mrs P and I have stopped looking for trucks with chains on even one wheel to lessen the danger of crossing Zoji La. We have given up scrounging food. We have abandoned all attempts at hygiene and we have now turned to prayer. One reason for coming to India was to find a guru who would clue us up about enlightenment. Well, we're certainly getting enlightenment. We want to go home soonest to try it out. We never want to set foot south of Haslemere again. Enlightened Rule One – Foreign Parts are for Foreigners.

I may as well tell you about Drass. It has one street, three dwellings loosely classified as hotels and no women. Yaks, dzos, goats, dogs, men in shaggy blankets yes, but no women. I read somewhere that in the interests of birth control polyandry is common in Ladakh. Having lived in Drass I can see why, though where the lucky women were I never found out.

I ran into the Chief of Police one morning standing beside his yak.

'Do you think I might borrow a typewriter anywhere?' I said.

'You must ask the office manager of the Drass Development Corporation,' he said, indicating a squatting, blanketed figure next to another yak.

'Please may I borrow your typewriter?' I said.

The office manager of the Drass Development Corporation considered the question in silence.

'How long for?' he said.

'An hour?' I said.

'Fifty minutes,' he said.

'Thank you,' I said.

We went to a concrete building with a mud floor and a ladder. We climbed the ladder and found an ancient machine on the floor. Five male secretaries, also in blankets, appeared to be guarding it. The office manager shouted orders in Hindi. Two secretaries carried the typewriter to a table, another brought a chair. The rest watched. I sat down. They waited.

'There is just one thing,' I said timidly. 'May I have some paper?'

'You did not ask for paper,' said the office manager accusingly.

This was true.

'You see, I can't really type without paper,' I explained.

'I have no spare paper,' said the office manager.

'Only a few sheets, say four,' I pleaded.

'Three,' said the office manager and unlocked a big tin cupboard.

I began to write a letter home. I told the children where I was and why, and how treacherous the road over Zoji La would be. I said I might not be home till the spring because in five days' time the road closed officially until May. Over my shoulder, the secretaries watched the letter grow. It was when I got to the part about doing their homework that I began to sniff. My glasses misted over, the words jumbled up. The sniffs became snivels, the keys jammed. It was no good. I abandoned all restraint, threw my head down and howled huge, heaving, choking, gasping, soggy sobs. The secretaries waited. After about ten minutes I stopped.

'You are weeping because there is something wrong with the machine?' asked the office manager.

Every morning we asked the captain if the road was open and every morning he said it was too dangerous for civilians. On the fourth day Mrs P and I sneaked out to the army camp and begged a lift. No permission, said the soldiers. I began to snivel anew.

'I have never seen an English lady weep,' said a soldier with interest. 'OK, get in, but you must lie down and stay quiet because I am carrying explosives and it is forbidden to take passengers. Please do not smoke.'

I can't tell you much about crossing Zoji La because I was lying in the back of the truck face down on top of a crateful of grenades covered by old sacks. It took eight hours to drive five vertical kilometres. Whenever we ran into a half-buried, defunct truck we squeezed past it, our chainless wheels inches from the edge. At midnight we reached the village of Sonemarg. The proprietor of the Dreamland Hotel locked us in our room because, he said, an English girl had been murdered here last month.

The flight from Leh to Srinagar takes an hour. We had been on the road for eight days. In the taxi to the Oberoi Palace Hotel I removed the two plastic carrier bags which I had been wearing over my feet in lieu of socks. Imagine Pandora's Box full of mature Stilton and last year's slurry and you will know the score when I removed the bags.

'Susan,' said Mrs P, running her fourth bath. 'Promise me that if I ever mention foreign travel again you will say one thing to me – Zoji La. OK?'

'OK,' I said.

Dinner with Donald

Once upon a time there was a perfectly sweet little duckling called Donald, though being a perfectly sweet little *French* duckling he answered to De Nalde and took four hours over his lunch.

Now De Nalde and his six fluffy yellow siblings grew up on a perfectly beautiful farm about a hundred miles south-west of Paris, lovingly tended by a farmer's wife with apple cheeks and a farmer with a large government subsidy. Every morning De Nalde's mother, Daffy (known as Mère d'Afie), led her brood out of the farmyard into the big field beyond, through which burbled two perfectly crystal clear and apparently identical streams. Off they waddled, *toute la famille*, quacking merrily, and like the 597,516 other ducks before them that had been reared there since 1890, they crossed the first stream looking neither to right nor left, clambered out the other side, sped across the field and with one united 'QUACK!' plunged into the second stream where they snapped at the flies, dive-bombed the bugs and, above all, gobbled up quantities of the delicious weed sprouting from either bank.

Thus they safely grazed until around 4.30, when the shadows began to lengthen, and at last Mère d'Afie looked up from her tadpole *digestif* and summoned her family. Led by De Nalde, fattest of the ducklings, they clambered out of the stream and formed themselves into time-honoured diagonal lines. Like statues they waited. Stock still. Not a feather stirring. Slowly the minutes ticked by (Proust would have liked this bit) and then as soon as the shadow of the tallest poplar touched the far gate-post, a slight breeze rose from the south-west, gently at first but getting stronger.

The ducklings spread their wings and allowed the wind to blow through their feathers, pinions rising and falling rhythmically like gymnasts limbering up. Exactly thus had the 597,516 other ducks behaved. As suddenly as it had risen the wind died away. The ducklings lowered their wings, stood at ease and followed Mère d'Afie back to the farmyard for the night.

Early next morning the apple-cheeked farmer's wife came tripping out of the farmhouse with a big bucket of corn. She called the ducklings by name, scattered the corn among them, and while they were busy scoffing she seized De Nalde by his yellow feet, took him behind the barn and wrung his neck.

'Pardon, Madame,' murmured a voice behind me, and one of the seven waiters hovering about our table handed me a card which said at the top, '*Le numéro de votre canard –* 597,517 (*depuis* 1890).'

Of course you've guessed. I am at that legendary restaurant in Paris called the Tour d'Argent where the speciality of the house is the numbered duck. I am not so befuddled with Kir Royale that I have dreamt up all that stuff about the two streams and the windy wing-waggling. It is all perfectly true, for I have just spent half an hour over my pre-prandial drink talking to the restaurant's equally legendary proprietor, Claude Terrail. With a perfectly straight face M. Terrail has assured me that every one of the 597,516 ducks (mine was still in the oven) served in his restaurant in the last ninety-one years has owed its exquisite flavour, its incontrovertible *je ne sais quoi*, to the unique conditions of its upbringing.

Only the weed from the second stream gave the flesh its distinctive tang, said M. Terrail. Once, to experiment, the weed from the first stream had been fed to ducks number 234,567 to 234,578 and the result had been *un désastre*. As for that curious wind, it had, said my host, refilling my glass, exactly the right force behind it to exercise the ducks' wings, thereby producing precisely the right muscular density, size and weight for his famous dish, Canard Nôtre Dame. The Tour d'Argent overlooks Nôtre Dame.

'It is quite extraordinary, but it is all perfectly true,' he concluded, shrugging his shoulders and spreading his hands wide.

'I do not doubt a word of it,' I said.

We ordered Canard Nôtre Dame and all the trimmings. Like his majestic predecessor Henry IV, duck number 597,517 came in two parts. Part I was a succulent affair, sauce-covered, and eaten with a shovel-shaped spoon. Part II, on a different plate, was its unadorned thighs.

M. Terrail stood confidently behind my chair and raised his eyebrows. 'Perfection, absolute perfection,' I breathed reverently.

'Wonderful, quite wonderful, especially the potatoes,' murmured my companion, who is Irish.

Of one thing alone I am certain. An un-numbered duck shall never pass my lips again.

Saturday night heaver

Every Saturday night, come hell or high water (preferably the latter) a boat leaves England for Holland with a cargo of writhing couples bent on completing a twenty-four disco-dance marathon. I know, because I've just done it.

Halfway over we ran into a Force 10 gale, which made the outward journey less 'Saturday Night Fever' than 'Saturday Night Heaver'. Casualties were high. However, I survived – just – and live to tell the tale.

Why anyone should voluntarily undertake such an ordeal and, what is more, pay good money to do so, defeats me. No entirely sane person would commit themselves to dance for twenty-four hours on terra firma, let alone on the high seas. But, as they say, there's one born every minute, and a good three hours' worth of loonies had booked for this particular voyage. So popular is the venture, in fact, that the disco ship has been booked solid since September.

The return trip was £10, couchettes or cabins extra, and drinks cost 45p a shot, which wasn't much to boogie about.

At least half the boppers came from Luton. I daresay the local Odeon had had a re-run of *They Shoot Horses, Don't They?* which fired the local girls to out-dance Miss Fonda.

Youth was the keyword. Most of the dancers who left Sheerness with me were around eighteen. There were two office outings (female) and several groups of swaggering lads with slicked-down, brushed-back, grease-soaked hair. The girls wore white sling-backs with six-inch heels. The boys wore sneakers with red and orange laces. There were a few elderly passengers, like me and the three German matrons built like barges who said, 'Die Boomen Town Rats? Vass iss Die Boomen Town Rats?' These were not disco participants, merely motorists on their way home.

The *Olav Kent*, a Danish vessel smelling strongly of herring, steamed out of Sheerness at half-past nine in the evening. Within ten minutes the Olympiads had taken up their positions on the disco deck, sling-backs to port, sneakers to starboard. I monitored the action from the safety of a bar-stool. First on the floor were two typists from Stevenage who jerked gracelessly to 'Stayin' Alive' and shouts of 'Sock it to 'em, Cheryl!' from supporters.

'Why aren't you dancing?' I asked a group of lads drinking Pernod and ginger ale. One had a bath towel round his neck – a wise virgin. His name was Trevor.

'Not enough room,' said Trevor. 'I gotta have room to mix it!'

'Why don't you ask the girls to dance?'

'We don't dance with girls,' said Trevor's mate patiently, as if he were explaining contraception to his granny. 'Girls are for decoration, see. They got to look good, dress good, a bit flash, walk good, parade a bit. We dance solo 'cos we've been practising the act at home on our own.'

'What do you think of the talent so far?' I asked a ginger-headed lad from Dunstable, who admitted to being a rubber goods apprentice.

'Rubbish,' he said, casting a discerning eye over the Stevenage sirens. 'Useless. Haven't got a clue, any of 'em. You should see some of the girls up the disco at Welwyn. Proper little ravers they are – psychedelic hair, satin pants, silver boots, the works. They wouldn't give you the time of day, mind, but they sure as hell know how to dress.'

At 10.15 Trevor, with the slow deliberation of Achilles emerging from his tent, handed his bath-towel to a second. He pushed back two tables adjoining the dance floor. His cronies watched with silent respect, the car passengers with apprehension. Trevor mixed it. His style was part cossack, part turbo-prop. He leapt, kicked, rolled, flailed, collapsed, revived and finally, after thirty-five minutes non-stop motion, exited towards the Gents.

And so it went on. And on. And on. Around midnight I was seduced from my stool just as the weather changed. I pitched and tossed dutifully for an hour, goaded on by the hoarse raving of the resident DJ, before lurching below to my cabin. The Stevenage girls, their numbers slightly depleted, were soldiering on in shifts. Those who weren't dancing lay groaning under the tables.

'Where's Trevor?' I asked.

'Throwing up in the couchettes,' said Trevor's mate.

At six next morning we reached Flushing, which seemed appropriate. At seven a.m. we were ordered ashore and herded on to a coach in the pitch dark for a scenic tour of the Dutch equivalent of Redhill and Reigate. At eight o'clock we were herded off the coaches into a sort of drill-hall for coffee and our first glimpse of a real live Dutchman, the only native awake at that hour. On the drive back to Flushing I counted eleven windmills and three industrial tips. By ten we were back on board, the turntables were spinning, and the Travoltas and Newton-Johns were back in business.

'Did you like it?' I asked Trevor at Sheerness, as he and the Luton bus were pulling out.

'Fantastic,' said Trevor. 'I've never been abroad before. For two pins I'd do it again tonight.'

Lucky chap. I don't think my two pins would make it.

Just good friends

When in Rome, they say, so naturally when in New York I went to see an analyst. After six days of breakfast television, singles bars and an evening at the Lone Star Café with three urban cowboys from Alabama and a simulated bucking bronco with a one-to-ten turbulence rating, I needed one.

'Can you recommend an analyst?' I asked the hotel receptionist.

'Certainly, madam. The Berkowitzes are very popular, I understand.'

Bernie and Mildred Berkowitz consolidated their reputation a few years back by bringing out a volume, not so much slim as anorexic (being all of seventy-seven pages long), called *How to be Your Own Best Friend*. They sold the paperback rights for something in excess of 800,000 dollars, which presumably made them their own best friends as well, a relationship further strengthened by the fact that it and its two sequels have been on international best-seller lists ever since.

Bernie was head-shrinking out of town that day, but Mildred Newman, as she is known professionally, received me in her penthouse apartment, heated to a temperature that would have daunted Abednego and his pals. Ms Newman is small, substantial and disarmingly friendly, and had buttoned her shirt up on the wrong buttons so that the left side hung four inches lower than the right. I wondered if this was significant – Miss Newman studied psychology under the late Theodore Reik – but it turned out to be a simple oversight.

We passed through a series of sumptuous rooms into a small pink study. I asked her what it was about New York that sent people racing in droves to see analysts. Miss Newman was precariously balanced on a small stool, searching on the top shelf of the bookcase for the Chinese edition of *How to be Your Own Best Friend*, and said absentmindedly that it was probably untrue that more New Yorkers went to analysts than anywhere else, and the truth was more likely that there were just more people *in* New York, so it looked that way.

I asked what made people in New York go to analysts, was it stress or loneliness or boredom or status? Ms Newman eventually located the Chinese edition, along with the Japanese, Finnish and Swahili editions, and descended. She said most of her clients felt they could do more with their lives and sought her advice as to how to go about it. This was easy because we all have the answer within ourselves already.

She also said that when the US broke off relations with Iran a reporter from *Time* magazine had been to interview the departing Iranian ambassador in Washington and there were just two things on his desk – his diary and a copy of *How to be Your Own Best Friend*. I obediently tucked the English, American and Punjabi editions into my handbag and asked if there was a simple solution to getting more out of one's life.

Ms Newman was now squatting on the floor looking in a cupboard for the Spanish and Gujerati editions. She said the secret was self-approval. Take the other day. She woke up and decided to give a beautiful party for her favourite uncle. She worked *so* hard. She made a fine dinner, set a beautiful table, made her apartment so welcoming. The morning of the party her uncle calls her. 'Hi Mil,' he says. 'Say, can you invite the So-and-sos along too?' Ms Newman does not like the So-and-sos.

'So what do I do? If I say no, I will make my uncle sad. If I pretend not to care and say yes I make myself sad because I do not approve of myself. So here's what I do. "Lookee uncle," I say. "I do not like the So-and-sos but I will invite them. My dinner will be a little ruined, my table will not be quite as beautiful or my apartment as welcoming, but I will do it for you." You see? You must *like* yourself.'

I found myself liking Ms Newman so much that we continued our conversation over lunch at a restaurant called the Library, whose walls were lined with books. I left two copies of *How to be Your Own Best Friend* on the shelf behind me next to *Middlemarch*. I like to spread a little happiness where I can.

Going home to Burma

'You have American dollars?' whispered a small man in a green lungi, sidling up crabways as I emerged from the Customs Hall of Rangoon airport. 'I give good price.'

'No,' I said.

'You have whisky, cigarettes?'

'Look,' I said, 'I don't want to sell anything. Please go away, I'm trying to find my uncle.'

At this a figure detached itself from the small crowd waiting to meet the Bangkok flight, a snake-like man with gleaming slicked-down hair and a huge purple wart over his left eyebrow. 'Did you say you were looking for your uncle?

You must be Susan. I am your Uncle Maurice. Welcome to Burma.'

'I haven't got an Uncle Maurice,' I said, consulting my list of long-lost and never-before-encountered relations. 'I'm expecting Uncle Johnny, or at least U Than Sein from Botataung.'

'Yes, yes, I know all that,' said Uncle Maurice, taking my arm and guiding me to a row of wooden seats in the middle of the hall. 'I am your *half*-uncle. We are all here. Your Uncle Johnny, your Auntie Amah, your cousins Irene, Olive, Kitty, Patricia – here she is,' he called out, and for the first time in my life I found myself in possession of relations. Real relations. Blood relations. When for thirty-odd years you have had but one father, one mother and one sister, the sudden addition of one and a half uncles is a sobering experience. I sat down.

Uncle Johnny, a paler, taller, sterner version of my father, in blue shirt and blue checked lungi, introduced me to a row of female cousins who spoke no English but giggled prettily behind their fingers like extras from *The Mikado*. Auntie Amah kept her handkerchief pressed tightly to her mouth not, I afterwards discovered, through an excess of emotion but because she had recently had all her teeth removed and was waiting for replacements.

Well, my mother had warned me there were certain shortages in Burma, which is why I was laden with handbags, lipstick, Ponds cold cream, St Michael sweaters, lighters and, above all, chocolate. There is no chocolate in Burma; the Burmese way to socialism does not include chocolate. Uncle Johnny explains that my other aunts, uncles, cousins, second cousins, in-laws, nephews and nieces are all waiting at home.

Before proceeding any further, I had better provide a few essential footnotes. Although I boast freely of being half-Burmese – both my grandmothers were Burmese, both my grandfathers pukka Brits – I have never actually *been* to Burma. My mother left when the Japanese invaded, making the terrible six-week trek by road to India with my elder sister, then three months old. I was born there, on an army camp near Dehra Dun, whence we eventually removed to England. For as long as I can remember our only contact with the folks back home was the annual handmade, spangly Christmas cards postmarked 'Southern Shan States' with their wonderful round Burmese script. I found it slightly strange that they sent cards, since I thought they were all Buddhists.

My friend and travelling companion knew a great deal more about my mother country than me, and during the fourteen-hour flight to Bangkok, she filled me in with some useful facts. To wit – Burmese script is rounded because it was originally written on palm leaves, any straight sharp stroke would tear the leaf; Burma has 33 million people, 10 per cent of whom are *pongyis* or Buddhist monks; *pongyis* are allowed five worldly possessions: orange robe, sandals, sun umbrella, fan and begging bowl. My mother had alerted me to two major social aspects of Burmese life, modesty and *ar nar de*. To conform to the former, we should not go see-through or strapless. As for *ar nar de*, it is one of those untranslatable words which means, roughly, extreme consideration and a reluctance to cause inconvenience to anyone. *Toujours la politesse* comes near.

Rangoon with its scorched red earth, its jacarandas, and hot heavy scents is overwhelmingly foreign, spine-tinglingly exotic. Men and women wear the classic lungi skirt which gives them a graceful languid gait. There are no beggars, no offensive sights or smells as there are in neighbouring India, nor the ubiquitous, obsequious smile so famous in hyper-commercial Thailand. The Burmese are gentle, dignified and incurious.

To be a tourist in Burma is to be in a hurry. A tourist visa lasts a week and if you want to do justice to the country and its culture this doesn't leave much slack. 'But I'm not a tourist, I'm a son of the soil returning to my roots,' I appealed to the Embassy in London.

Seven days, they said, and with a new passport stating '*Occupation: housewife*' (journalists have a hard time getting into Burma), I had arrived in Rangoon to start searching. I met innumerable uncles, aunts and cousins on my father's side and dined at the home of my mother's cousin, a former ambassador, where we drank sweet champagne at a teak Formica-topped table and heard his wife complain about the servants (Rangoon isn't so different from Reigate).

On our way to the airport we stopped at Monletsaunggon – Pudding Lane – to see my mother's younger sister, Auntie Betty. Monletsaunggon is a noisy, colourful, down-at-heel neighbourhood: children made mud pies in the road, women squatted over wooden bowls, the wood houses were crammed close together, clothes lines on every veranda. Number 12 was a fragile house divided into flats.

'Where is Daw Sein Ohn?' They point upwards and we climb an outside staircase to a dim room with an assortment of furniture – deck chairs, camp chairs, stools, pots, baskets and heaps of clothes lying about. A young girl in trousers comes towards us, our guide speaks to her in Burmese and she disappears behind a curtain. A man emerges, smoothing back his tousled hair as if he has just woken up. He is small, spare, ageless, and to me he appears as foreign as a Tuareg or Inca.

'You are Marjorie's daughter. I am Uncle Sein Ko. Please sit. We will fetch your Auntie Betty.'

It is all too much. My eyes prick and Gail, my companion, is noisily blowing her nose. My new family stand waiting politely and a little puzzled at the two strange ladies with head colds. Auntie Betty arrives apologetic, *ar nar de*, and the photo album is produced. For the first time I see a picture of my grandmother, looking uncannily like Queen Victoria in a lungi.

And now we are heading north to the beautiful hill station at Taung-gyi, where the people are no longer Burmese but Shan, and where our closest family ties lie. When she heard of my proposed visit, Auntie May wrote and asked if I would bring a hot-water bottle to keep her hands warm in church. Of course – she and my mother went to the English mission school at Moulmein. Auntie May has retained the faith and every Christmas her small Buddhist grandchildren sing 'Silent Night' round the Christmas tree.

We turn a corner and drive slap into a fairy tale. A long procession of ponies, gorgeously apparelled, is coming towards us. On each sits a small boy dressed like a king. They wear golden crowns, gold stars are painted on their faces, their costumes are heavy with flowers and jewels and bells, and beside each walks an adult attendant holding a lacquer umbrella over the potted potentate's head. What on earth – of course, it is a *shin byu*, the Buddhist equivalent of a first communion. For three months the child will live like a real *pongyi* – shaved head, orange robe, begging bowl.

Behind the ponies comes a lorry so crowded with people that the vehicle is invisible. A small space has been cleared on the back and a *pwe* is in full tilt. Literally, a *pwe* is a demonstration of Burmese dancing. The reality is impossible to describe. In Bangkok we saw classical Thai dancers in stiff elaborate costumes moving so delicately, so woodenly. The dancer on the back of the truck is not wood, she is fire – a child of about ten with a mane of tangled hair and a small glowing face. Like quicksilver she leaps, arches, pirouettes, her palms stretched back towards her wrists like soaring birds, her feet tossing up the hem of her lungi like flames licking round dry logs. It is magic, pure magic. We stand by the roadside – villagers, children, chickens, dogs and two large black pigs. At last, ponies and *pwe* disappear round the corner and we return to our jeep. It seems very quiet, very empty and a little sad.

When I walk into the lobby and see Auntie May it is like seeing my mother in Burmese dress. It isn't just that she speaks perfect English (for forty years she has taught English in the front room of her house); her whole demeanour, her carriage, her *air* are European. Those English missionaries who taught my mother and her elder sister in Moulmein certainly did a thorough job.

We order tea and immediately Auntie May starts firing a lifetime's worth of questions like a succession of darts. How old are my children, how many are at school, are they clever, how is my sister, when is her baby due? She sits next to me, so alert, so impatient, so un-Burmese, in her pale lungi and a thick Arran cardigan (sent by my mother years ago), her tiny hands clasped in her lap, that she could easily be one of those delicate ivory statuettes.

'I should like to see your Mummy again. Is she well?'

'She's fine. When did you last see her?'

'On the morning of 8 December 1941, the day after Pearl Harbour. When I came home in the evening your Mummy had gone. Your grandmother was weeping. "Where is Marjorie?" I asked her. "She has gone to Mandalay with the other officers' wives, she has taken the baby," said your grandmother. And then your Mummy did the trek to India with your sister and I never saw her again. Tell me, is she still so pretty?'

Going to market with her is like going on a magical mystery tour. Women from the hill villages sit on the ground in front of huge baskets overflowing with – with what? Heaven knows what those strange mud-coloured cakes are, or those long fronded vegetables or those tiny brick-coloured beans. I've never seen so many kinds of bean. Auntie May talks all the time.

We have tea at a tobacco factory where, in a large airy room, girls sit cross-legged on the ground, sorting cheroot-wrapping leaves in sizes as if they are dealing a hand of poker. We eat lunch in Auntie May's schoolroom, where one of her grandchildren has written on the blackboard 'Welcome To Our Humble Home'. There are photos on the wall of all eleven grandchildren and of my sister graduating from St Andrew's. We eat *kauk-swe* and *mon-hin-ga* and *let-thok* (coconut rice, noodles, shrimps and garlic), and as we eat Auntie May's daughter stands behind her mother swishing away flies with a palm leaf fan, not obsequiously like a punkah wallah but with the respect that comes naturally to the Burmese for the elders.

'And tell me, Susan, what does your husband do?' asks my aunt.

'He is a stockbroker.'

'What is a stockbroker?'

'Well, he takes other people's money and puts it in stocks and shares, to make it grow into more money,' I say, struggling with what to me too is a pretty esoteric art. 'He tries to make people richer.'

Auntie May leans forward, her eyes wide. 'Is that *legal*?' she says.

Taung-gyi to Mandalay is a ten-hour drive, growing hotter and dustier as we near the central plains. We pass trees with huge crimson flowers – the Flame of the Forest – and farmers ploughing behind yoked bullocks with big black umbrellas held above their heads as sunshades. We stop at tea houses where the tea is free and slowly, politely (for the Burmese are the politest people on earth), we talk to the other passengers.

At Mandalay my cousin Aye-Aye-Maw, who is studying maths at university, meets us and takes us to a friend's house for tea. We go into a cool dim room where a crowd of children are watching cartoon films on a colour television set which is still in its cardboard box. Television came to Burma last year.

Next morning on our way to the pagoda we are stuck in a traffic jam, a delightful experience since the traffic consists of bicycles, horse-drawn rickshaws and a few elderly Hillmans. We wash and wish to gain merit and kneel at the feet of the great golden Maha-muni, one of only five life portraits of the Lord Buddha. There are two more in India and the last two are in Paradise.

We visit the incomparable Kaung-hmu-daw Pagoda built by a former king as an exact replica of his wife's breast, dazzling white in the sun. White is a sacred colour in Burma. In olden days if you found a white elephant you were exempt from paying taxes for life; only kings could ride white elephants.

We take a boat down the Irrawaddy, the wide wonderful Irrawaddy, and stop at a sandbank for watermelon. A woman brings a watermelon the size of a bicycle wheel and Aye-Aye-Maw launches into a financial deal. We pick up the water-melon, we exclaim, we smile and we eventually settle at eight *kyats*. Everyone is happy.

Back in Rangoon, we have an invitation to dine with Mr Fenn, the British ambassador. We step into a grey vintage Daimler and are swept away to a magnificent old colonial house built originally for the manager of the Irrawaddy Flotilla company. A Burmese cat stalks through the door ahead of us and a Bach oratorio is flooding the ante-ante-room. Mrs Fenn, cool, blonde and beautiful in sugar-pink organza, rises from a deep sofa to greet us. Our man in a short-sleeved shirt, Nicholas Fenn, tells us that Rangoon was his first diplomatic posting twenty years earlier and ever since then he and Susan, his wife, had been trying to winkle their way back. They both speak fluent Burmese.

Burma, says Mr Fenn without a trace of pomposity or patronage, is a blushing flower surrounded by weeds – he tactfully declined to mention India, Bangladesh, Laos, China and Thailand – which threaten to choke it. It needs protecting but it is quite simply the most beautiful, unspoilt country on earth. I'll drink to that.

Alone and palely loitering

'We could go to singles bar to start with,' said my friend Leina. 'New York is full of them. It would be a good place for you to observe big city *mores*.'

But we're dreary old married ladies,' I said.

'So is everyone who goes to singles bars really,' said Leina. 'P. J. Clark's is good straight from the office – it gets full of ad men and media executives around 6.30. Or we could leave it till later and try Maxwell Plum.'

'Is it straight singles or gay singles?' I asked nervously. I was finding New York candidly and disconcertingly homosexual. Going down in the hotel lift on my first night I was invited for a drink by a woman of around forty in khaki slacks, called Prentiss. She had heard I was British and wanted to know about genealogists. Prentiss bought me a marguerita with extra salt and then suggested we go down to the Village to a grocery store called Food. I said I didn't want any groceries. Prentiss said Food was a great meeting ground for gays. I bought her a drink and said I wasn't gay and when she left she said she'd call me sometime.

'No. Maxwell Plum is pretty straight,' said Leina. 'See you there at nine.'

The bar was dim and crowded and vaguely art deco. The women were casually elegant and talked with great animation and plenty of expansive gestures. The men wore sports jackets and frequently fingered their wallets.

I learnt afterwards that the crucial moment in a singles bar is the moment you step in the door, because you have to decide who you're going to make for. Leina and I made for the nearest empty space at the bar. We ordered drinks. There were bowls of popcorn on the counter.

'What are the gals drinking?' It was the dark, heavily built middle-aged man on my right. 'Give them a coupla Canadian clubs,' he said to the barman. He took out a huge wodge of $20 bills and started riffling through them as if he were looking up a telephone number.

Leina said graciously, 'Thank you very much. Do you come here often?' I was deeply impressed by this social panache.

'You bet, sugar. My name's Ron Pacelli. Cheers.'

The small thin fellow on Leina's left engaged her in badinage, which left me on my own with Ron. He had moved appreciably closer.

'Where do you live, Ron?' I asked pathetically.

'Where do you think I live, sugar?' he replied.

Now I know American cars have clues on their number-plates like 'The home of great potatoes', which means Idaho or something, but I didn't know they had clues on their persons too. I looked hard at Ron's tie, Ron's shirt, Ron's trousers and Ron's jacket.

'Like it?' said Ron stroking the sleeve of his jacket with one hand and the sleeve of my jacket with the other. 'Two hundred and twenty-five dollars from Bloomingdale's last fall – 100 per cent velour velvet. OK, let's see. I live in Philadelphia, six room duplex, wrap around terrace, one and a half baths, I've got a Chevvy Malibu cabriolet round the block and I wanna move back to New York City.'

'What's half a bath?' I asked.

Ron looked surprised. 'Closet and vanity in back,' he said mysteriously.

He was now leaning heavily against me, breathing hard.

'Let me buy *you* a drink, Ron,' I said, wedging my handbag between us. 'And what do you do in Philadelphia?'

'What do you think I do, sugar?' said Ron. Here we go again. He turned out to be some kind of salesman but he preferred that we should talk about us. There was nothing, said Ron, absentmindedly searching for his lighter in the inside pocket of his $225 jacket, that he liked better than the company of an intimate and sensuous woman. He himself was also highly sensuous, being a Scorpio. What was I? A Virgo, he'd bet on it? Listen, why didn't we get into his Chevvy Malibu cabriolet and ride around awhile? Maybe go to a casino in Atlantic City?

I pulled at Leina's sleeve. She smiled with unnatural brilliance and said, 'This is Greg. He's an accountant but he really wants to concentrate on sculpture. He lives in Manhattan but wants to move to Philadelphia with his folks.'

'This is Ron,' I said. 'He lives in Philadelphia but wants to move to Manhattan.'

'Hi, Ron,' said Greg.

'Hi, Greg,' said Ron. We left them together.

Singles bars can be very useful, I said to Leina in the cab on our way back to the hotel.

Aloha, m'sieur

I had a letter the other day covered with big balloon-shaped stamps like a nursery frieze and bearing the postmark Nuku Alofa. This surprised me as I didn't know I knew anyone in Nuku Alofa. It was from my mother, who lives in Sussex.

The weather, she wrote, had been so disappointing this year that she and my father had rented their house in Brighton to a man connected with double glazing and had in turn rented themselves a thatched dwelling without double glazing (or for that matter any glazing at all) in Tongatapu, principal island of the archipelago that composes the independent Kingdom of Tonga.

My mother went on to describe the state of her refrigerator, how to cook salt fish in banana leaves and the habits of her new next-door neighbour, King Tanfa Ahun Tupon IV, with whom, it seems, she shares a milkman. Last Sunday morning she saw King Tanfa strolling out of the Royal Palace on his way to church (he is a Wesleyan) wearing a yellow crash helmet.

'Why is the King wearing a yellow crash helmet?' she asked the Palace guard, whom she had called in to mend her refrigerator.

'His Majesty is always being presented with ceremonial hats by visiting dignitaries,' replied the guard, 'and he likes to wear a different one every day.'

I did not intend to write about Tonga this week. My text was to be nearer home, namely the vicissitudes of the hotel trade and how to succeed therein. I have just, for reasons too complicated and delightful to go into at present, been staying at the George V in Paris, a gem's throw from the Champs Elysées and arguably one of the Great Hotels of the World.

If President Mitterrand is scaring the *pantalons* off the wealthier citizens of France with his threats of austerity measures, the George V hasn't yet heard the news. There was nothing very austere about the languorous Argentinian lady sitting in the foyer dripping Cartier and surrounded by fourteen pieces of crocodile luggage, nor the trolley piled with *saumon fumé* and Krug trundling up the corridor to a private suite.

177

Why is it, I thought, tipping Nina Ricci into my bath, that only the French know about style? Why is it, I mused, switching on the Baccarat chandelier above my bed, that only the French excel in elegance? But what was this? The slim, dark young man behind the gilded reception desk, a look-alike for the Gitanes ad, who with typical Gallic gallantry offered to show me some of the newly refurbished *chambres*, came from Reading. His name was David.

'What's a nice young man like you doing in a place like this?' I asked as he ushered me with disturbing deference into the marble and gold leaf of the President's suite.

David said he had been lucky to get the job because he had no proper qualifications, no Ordinary National Diploma or Hotel Management degree. Instead of hot-footing to Reading tech to gain these dubious honours he had written to all the big hotel companies for a job. All but the Savoy group had told him to run along and get his diploma and come back in three years' time.

The Savoy knew better. They took him on. For a year he worked in the kitchens of Simpson's in the Strand, for another he was a floor waiter at the Berkeley Hotel, then a stint in the administrative offices of Claridge's, some bar work at Stone's Chop House and eventually reception at the Savoy. He has been at the George V for two years. His French is immaculate.

But what could you possibly learn at Reading tech that you haven't picked up from experience, I asked, sinking to my armpits in blue damask.

Portion control, plate appeal, menial and social duties, said David. He personally had never had to be taught social conduct. The last person to occupy this suite, he said, passing into the Presidential bedroom with its vast bed whose counterpane could have doubled as a swimming pool cover, was the King of Tonga, an enormous man, twenty-seven stone and closing on seven feet. On arrival he had shaken

David's hand, crushing every bone, but David, without the benefit of an OND in Hotel Management, had not flinched.

'Did you say the King of Tonga,' I cried excitedly as if he had mentioned an old friend. 'I know him. He lives next to my mother. What did he have on his head?'

David registered no surprise. A trilby, he thought. He also said they had had to add another three feet to the bottom of the bed to accommodate the royal guest. The King had particularly liked the electronic panel that operated the TV and the chamber maid and spent some time making the window blinds go up and down very fast.

'You mentioned mass at Nôtre-Dame,' murmured David leading me to the lift. 'Perhaps we should be making a move . . .'

I swear if that young man, diplomas notwithstanding, isn't general manager of the Villa d'Este in ten years time, I'll eat the King of Tonga's crash helmet.

Divorce bees-knees

I finally caught up with Dr Marcos von Goihman in Paris, by the south-eastern leg of the Eiffel Tower. He took me out to lunch, which set him back 300 dollars, but when you've got millions more stashed away in banks all over the monogamous world, who's counting pennies? I say monogamous because divorce is Dr von Goihman's business, or *bees-knees* as he calls it, being Uruguayan by birth and not unlike Mexican Pete of the comic strips in delivery and appearance. He stands four feet eleven inches in his cream silk socks.

What first attracted me to the good doctor was an advertisement in that well-known organ the *Times of Oman*. 'Divorce in 24 Hours' it read, and somewhere in the small print it mentioned a trip to the Caribbean as part of the package. Intrigued, I telephoned the Washington office for further details.

'Thees ees Dr Gonzales. You wanna getta twenty-four hour settlement?' said the voice 2–3,000 miles away.

'Well, not just yet,' I said. 'Can I speak to the boss?'

'Sure sure, you wanna try heem at the Athens Hilton, the Budapest Hilton, the Paris Hilton, the Tokyo Hilton. Dr von Goihman,' he added, unnecessarily I thought, 'is travelling.'

All this by way of prologue. The following act consisted of me and the diminutive doctor stuffing our faces with lobster and champagne in an intimate restaurant close to Nôtre-Dame. He at once produced two illustrated brochures, one outlining company business, the other showing pictures of his secretary, Susan, a pneumatic blonde, in a bikini.

Reluctantly I turned to official bees-knees. This is the deal. If you want an instant, no-messing divorce recognised by the Catholic church, the only place on earth you can get one is that sun-drenched Caribbean island split into Haiti and the Dominican Republic. Send 3,000 dollars and your papers to Dr von Goihman (deduct 100 dollars if it's an uncontested divorce) and he will fix you a return flight from New York, including overnight stay in a luxury hotel. Next morning you collect your decree nisi and fly home as free and unfettered as Mary Poppins. Until the next time round.

Dr von Goihman has had some repeat bookings. His Washington office, he says, handles 300 divorces a month from all over the world. The trickier ones he deals with personally, hence his foreign trips.

How Marcos (we had dispensed with formality by now) got into the divorce game is a tale as complex and unlikely as Scheherezade's. The chief influences in his hectic life appear to have been a one-legged uncle in Argentina, the director of a ladies' clothing store in Puerto Rico, an editor-in-chief of Time-Life and a Trust House Forte's receptionist. Somewhere along the line he served in the Israeli army, got a BA at Mississippi University, a law degree from Portugal and a taste for tall women. His ex-wife is five foot nine inches.

But how had he tied up the Caribbean business? Marcos explained. 'Twenny years ago the President Trujillo of Dominica he wanted a divorce real bad, real quick but he wanted a *Catholic* divorce. I cannot say eet for sure but he pay the Vatican one million dollar maybe two million dollar and he get it. All I do ees to buy the exclusive franchise on divorce in the island. I have ninety employees. I advertise in 346 newspapers. Maybe I advertise in the *Observer*. You wanna fix eet for me?'

In seven years Marcos von Goihman has cornered the divorce market. His clients, he says, include heads of state, ambassadors, Richard Burton and Jane Fonda. The caption under a photo of another satisfied client in the brochure reads thus: 'Although he is short and virtually one-eyed, Alan J. Lerner is also this country's most frequently married lyricist.' He assured me that a secretary from Kensington Palace sent for a brochure earlier this year.

Is the dynamic doctor a satisfied man? 'Listen, I speak you straight from the heart. I am thirty-seven years old. I am wealthy. I have three beautiful condominiums (luxury service apartments) in Argentina, Costa Rica and Virginia. But deep inside of me I am not a happy man. Always the wine in the afternoon he make me so sad. Listen. I have an idea. Why you no come up to my room, and I show you the peectures of my condominiums?'

Oh dear, Dr von Goihman, I'd love to but I've got to get the 7.19 to Gatwick, I think I said.

Le weekend

Scene: the Brasserie Alfred in Place Dalton, Boulogne-sur-Mer, the 11.30 hovercraft has just landed, disgorging the Arnolds and a full load of English day-trippers in blue quilted mail-order waistcoats or battered green Renaults, or both. Let us follow the family Pratt, Jeremy and Fiona and their two children Jasper and Barnaby, who live at Clapham (Common not Junction) and are enjoying a package-deal family weekend at the Dover Holiday Inn. It's incredibly good value, £39 per adult, bed and breakfast, nothing for the kids and all manner of extras – free T-shirts, playing cards, chocolates and, of course, the day trip to Boulogne. Actually, the Pratts almost didn't get to Boulogne because a couple of ferries had broken down, but Jeremy cut up rough with the booking clerk, pointing out quite reasonably that a weekend in Dover was not unlike a weekend at Heathrow, and eventually got his way. The Pratts are travelling with their friends Trevor and Valerie Leathers, who have moved from Clapham to the depths of the country, Dorking, with their two children Toby and Ophelia.

The hovercraft is an hour late and the famous not-to-be-missed Saturday morning market has just packed up. A refuse van is hosing down the picturesque cobbled square. It's a shame because Valerie was planning to buy a quantity of wonderful *légumes, mange-tout*, garlic, olives, and tons of proper *bouquets garnis*. When the Pratt party arrives at Alfred's (recommended in all the guide books, but Fiona knows it personally) all the tables, with their gay red check cloths, have been taken by the trippers from the 11.00 ferry. Everyone, with the exception of table 8, is English. Table 8 are Australians. The Pratts and the Leathers stand self-consciously in the narrow gangway between the tables and have to flatten themselves to one side when a peasant, in a merry *foulard*, comes in carrying a huge basket full of *baguettes* and everyone rushes forward with their Instamatics.

The patron, presumably Alfred, thin, elderly and wearing a crumpled grey suit, tells the Pratts to come back *dans une demi-heure*. Jeremy threatens to cut up rough again. '*Mais nous avons reservé une table pour huit personnes à une heure* precisely,' he says. Alfred indicates the packed tables – the Australians have managed to squeeze nine on to a table for four – and throws up his hands in a helpless gesture. Unfortunately, he happens to be carrying three bowls of *soupe de poissons* and a seafood salad at the time and Jeremy's quilted waistcoat is splattered with little pieces of interesting-looking fish. 'Never mind, darling,' says Fiona. 'We'll shoot off to Prisunic and stock up on plonk and cheese. I promised Marigold some *chèvre* for her dinner party on Tuesday.'

'*Alors, monsieur*,' says Jeremy to Alfred, who is now staggering by under a load of *moules marinières*. '*Nous irons maintenant mais nous reviendrons à deux heures* sharp.'

Trevor and Valerie decide to skip Prisunic in favour of a pavement café and two glasses of absinthe. Valerie says she doesn't feel she's really in France till she's had an absinthe. There are no pavement cafés in evidence, it has begun to drizzle, and the Leathers end up in a sort of fast food takeaway, sipping their absinthes, standing up next to a space invader machine. Toby and Ophelia wander about the Place Dalton kicking the picturesque cobblestones and wingeing for their lunch.

Prisunic is crammed with stuff that to a less discerning eye than Fiona's looks exactly like the stuff you can buy in Boots or Woolworth's. Fiona knows it is all just a little bit different – well, it's French after all – and buys a plastic parsley cutter, a wooden spoon and two pairs of knickers. Jeremy heads purposefully for the wine with his pocket calculator.

Back at Alfred's, a dispirited queue of day-trippers from the 11.30 Folkestone ferry is waiting. Alfred shows the Pratts and the Leathers to table 8, recently vacated by the Australians who have left seven empty wine bottles and an impressive collection of beer, wine and brandy glasses, full of floating cigarette butts and pieces of bread. The children demand fish fingers, but settle for *pommes frites* and ice-cream. The adults, except for Jeremy, order *coquilles St Jacques* and *sole bonne femme*. Jeremy has the speciality *fruits de mer* which arrives on a tray the size of a Citroen tyre and appears to have most of the Great Barrier Reef piled on it.

'I'll say one thing for the Frogs,' says Trevor, eating his sole in a noisy but typically French manner, 'they know how to cook seafood. Last business trip I had in Paris we went to this homosexual nightclub in Montparnasse and had the best bloody *langoustine* I've ever tasted.'

'Honestly, darling,' murmurs Fiona. '*Pas devant les enfants*, pleeeease.'

Three hours later, Jeremy is still chewing his way through half a hundredweight of crustacea. Barnaby, Ophelia and Toby have been banished to the car. 'I do so adore France,' says Valerie dreamily. 'It's so simple yet so civilised.'

Jeremy puts two kilos of shellfish into his Prisunic carrier bag and calls for four large armagnacs.

'When can we go back to the Holiday Inn?' says Jasper, moodily spooning garlic mayonnaise into his ice-cream. 'I hate abroad.'

Dior diary

On Monday I did the Impressionists. On Tuesday I was going to do the Mona Lisa, but she was closed. So after wandering dispiritedly round the Louvre for a while I thought I'd nip up to Dior in the Avenue Montaigne on the off-chance of picking up a little something in the sales for the Old Carthusian football club dance. Hang it all, if the gallant ship really is going down, as everyone keeps saying, I might as well be wearing my glad rags when it hits the bottom.

I had no idea the place was so vast. Dior is less a couture house than a couture megastore. I kept going into the wrong department. No thank you, I said, I won't have a set of matching tea towels or a £125 baby's romper suit embroidered with rabbits, although it is certainly *mignon*. A nice dress, please, I said to a salesman, something like that. I pointed to a ravishingly chic girl in scarlet.

'That is one of our sales assistants and she is wearing her uniform,' he replied kindly, and called her over. 'Madam would like to see the dresses,' he said.

The salesgirl led me with some urgency up a densely carpeted curving staircase that appeared to have been washed down that morning with Diorissima perfume. 'You must hurry,' she said, 'the show is just starting.'

We came to a room worthy of Chatsworth, dripping chandeliers and oozing Vivaldi. I was shown to a small gilt chair and given a programme marked 'Spring Collection'. There were two fierce ladies in the front row dressed in black, their iron-grey hair coiffed like cottage loaves and held in place with masonry nails. These, I was told, were extremely important and hugely influential ready-to-wear buyers. The chair next to me was reserved for Madame Yamaha, but she must have broken down somewhere. We were going to see 108 original ensembles designed by M. Marc Bohan, beginning with a pink silk mackintosh and matching shorts and ending with a patchwork evening gown in fuchsia and grey.

It was all breathtakingly exotic and a little removed from the Old Carthusian football club dance. The models were built like the Eiffel Tower, nine foot, six stone, legs like scaffolding and shoulders like Superman.

'Why are they so top-heavy?' I asked the woman in front, who was clearly a trendspotter as she was wearing her dress and necklace back to front.

'Padded shoulders are *de rigueur*,' she hissed, and broke off to clap excitedly as a black model wearing a cake frill and pearly queen pyjama bottoms stalked past.

I *quite* liked the coats cut like lopped-off science overalls, and I know that Sherpa Tensing would have been interested in all the enormous crêpe-de-chine anoraks with pockets ample enough to hold a sleeping bag and a change of thermal underwear, but what I really loved was the evening wear. M. Bohan is obsessed with milkmaids. The evening dresses had billowing tulip skirts overladen with Miss Muffet flounces and enough organdie in the ribbon-bows strapped on to their backsides to gift-wrap Nôtre-Dame. Heaven knows how you'd sit down in them or even get out of the front door, but why bother with details? Let us paint with broad brushes, gird our loins with sixteen metres of purple organdie ribbons, and make haste to the football club hop.

The audience were pretty dead-pan. I suppose they'd seen it all before. Years ago Dior had an American customer who didn't bother to come to the collections; she just ordered one of everything and let them get on with it. Only once did the two fierce ladies in the front row show any sign of emotion. It was for outfit number 92, a wildly complicated affair including black and white taffeta knickers, several overskirts, a jacket and some incidental frills. The cottage loaves nodded with approval and notes were taken. I bet Marks and Spencer will be selling taffeta knickers by the end of next week.

It was over. They switched off Vivaldi and the chandeliers, and one of the models passed me in the corridor wearing a dressing gown.

'Who can still afford a dress for £5,000?' I asked Alexandra from the upstairs office. Not many English women these days, she said, but a useful number of Brazilians, Americans, Japanese and of course Middle Eastern princesses. Up in the *flue*, the workrooms where the silk dresses are made, they were working on a wedding dress for a desert princess. Dotted around were the other tailors' dummies, each with the name of the customer and her personal Dior assistant written on the neck. There are going to be some tubby milkmaids doing the social rounds this year.

'And is one dress, albeit with the Dior *haute couture* label inside, really worth £5,000?' I asked. Alexandra shrugged. Every ensemble, she explained, involved at least 100 hours' work. Every stitch was hand-sewn, the garment was made on the customer's body, first in a sort of muslin meat-wrap material and then the real thing. In fact the profit margin was very low, only 2.5 per cent. No wonder poor M. Bohan has to flog himself to death designing tea towels and teddy bears to keep his head above water.

We passed another of the house models wearing patchwork shorts. She was very, very thin. Most of them are size eight or less. What happens, I asked Alexandra, hope rising in my size eight bosom, to the old, worn and distinctly secondhand outfits we'd seen on the catwalk that afternoon once the collections were over at the end of May? Were they chucked away, and if so where were the dustbins?

Alexandra said if you were quick enough you could reserve

a demonstration dress and buy it for half-price when the season was over. They don't offer HP terms. I've already asked.

Holy Rollers

What am I doing in the most expensive hotel in Seattle with a suitcase full of red clothes and a Farley's rusk? I am waiting for my friend Mrs P, veteran of many Arnold campaigns – Ladakh '81, Rangoon '83 – to fly in from Zürich so that we can resume where we left off three years ago on the Road to Enlightenment.

I am staying in this dazzlingly expensive hotel (when they learnt that I had no credit card of any kind, an incredulous frisson ran through the lobby, two bulky men appeared behind me, my room key was snatched from my hand and I was ordered to pay my bill immediately) because Mrs P's husband is here too, and international businessmen always stay in the best hotels.

My suitcase is full of red clothes because we are heading for the Big Muddy Ranch in Oregon, home for the past three years of that most extraordinary of gurus, Bhagwan Shree Rajneesh, of whom two things are generally known. First that his *sannyasins* wear clothes the colour of the rising sun, powder pink through to deep purple, and second that he collects Rolls-Royces as most of us collect safety pins, forty-seven at the last count. We are not, as yet, *sannyasins* but we want to be inconspicuous.

And the rusk is for wee Jim who, because this trip has been arranged at a moment's notice, has had to come too, in pink socks and orange pants. 'Are you sure you can manage with the baby?' asked the editor doubtfully.

'Of course. You know these communes, joy, brown rice, free love. Everyone will have babies. James is a vital prop.'

There is a knock at the door and a man enters carrying a tray. 'Ah thank heavens, that's my tea,' I say.

The waiter sets the tray down and stands belligerently in front of it. 'You're the cash customer, aren't you?' he says. 'That'll be 9.75 plus tax.'

I pour tepid water from a silver Thermos jug on to a teabag and think wistfully of Mother India, where we may have been thwarted in our attempt to find The Truth but at least you could get a decent cup of tea.

For those of you who have never heard of Bhagwan Shree Rajneesh, let me fill you in. He is fifty-two, a former theology professor from Bombay who became enlightened in 1961 and thereafter established an ashram in Poona to which questing folk from all over the world flocked to listen to his discourses. No one would deny that he attracted a nice class of quester, the rich, royal, rock-star type. One of Prince Charles's German cousins was Bhagwan's personal bodyguard. Converts to Rajneeshism received a new Indian name and a *mala* – a medallion with the Master's bearded visage inscribed on it.

Back in '81 Mrs P and I had Bhagwan high on our list of Sages-at-whose-feet-we-should-sit, but an early snowfall and ten days marooned in the mountains put paid to all that. In June of that year the Enlightened One suddenly and mysteriously left Poona and headed West with his disciples, the rich and royal and sundry others like my mother's window cleaner in Brighton, Chandra Dave; and since setting foot on American soil he has apparently taken a vow of silence.

I sympathise. There are aspects of American life that leave me speechless too, but what about his flock? Surely he had a duty to instruct them? Bhagwan has uttered more than 33 million words, says his head office. Thus all that needs to be said has been said already. Anyone wishing to clarify some nice theosophical point can refer to the aforementioned 33 million words, which have been lovingly transcribed into some 350 books in seventeen languages. As a literary superstar he's up there with H. Robbins and B. Cartland, who also favours pink. There may be a connection.

As for my own preoccupation with gurus and this one in particular, suffice to say that I go along with Rudolf Steiner who reckoned that at birth we're provided with enough inner petrol to keep rolling for half our lives. But come the mid-thirties, when we've done all our getting and spending, we need to turn inwards and ask whither and wherefore and why? My own tank is running low and the Rancho Rajneesh seems a cheerier place to fill up than some of these dry as dust holy men who want you to give everything up. The Perfect Rajneeshi, says Bhagwan, is a cross between Zorba and Buddha, someone who has vitality and lust for life as well as spiritual awareness. Yeah, that's the kind of thing I'm after.

Mrs P arrives. Yes of course we're going to Rajneeshpuram, she says, but first her husband has to do a little business. While we are waiting for him to complete a series of multi-million-dollar deals involving scrap iron in banana republics, we have use of a Chevrolet Silverado Suburban which is what you get when you cross a Rolls-Royce with a Green Line bus, and we stay in a resort area called Sun River. Every morning we go to Jazzercise dance classes beside the pool in the country club. Our neighbour's log cabin has a hangar instead of a garage so that when he flies up from San Diego at weekends he can jump straight from his plane into the pool. A fellow Jazzerciser tells me of two scientific breakthroughs. One is to do with improving the flavour of beef by injecting the carcasses with pawpaw juice to break down the fibre, and the other is an anti-nuclear device which

Boeing are working on in Seattle. 'It's really neat,' she says, rubbing sun oil on her thigh, 'it's like this big fan that screens off the city, and the Soviet missiles just hit up against it.'

We leave your luxury log cabin condominium with its built-in barbecue odour extractor in Sun River at dawn to drive the hundred or so miles to Rancho Rajneesh in time, we hope, for a quick pre-breakfast meditation. When you've only got three days to find Enlightenment you can't afford to hang about.

'Hey, you guys aren't seriously going to see that kooky guru with the forty-seven Rolls-Royces?' a man from Cinnamon Ridge had asked us at last night's odour-free barbecue.

'Yes,' we said.

'Well watch out they don't brainwash you,' advised Mrs Cinnamon Ridge, a bulky broad in satin pants. 'Our neighbour's daughter had a friend who joined this crazy Bhagwan cult. Once a month they let her out to have lunch. Then one day she says, "Carly honey, this is the last time I'm gonna have lunch with you. *They won't let me come any more.*"'

Driving through the early morning Oregon mist over the Deschutes River and past the Three Sisters mountains, I feel relieved I've brought wee Jim with me – it's impossible to brainwash someone with a five-month-old baby: they've already *been* brainwashed by womb-lag.

We leave the highway at a sign marked Cold Camp Road. The last 20 miles is on dirt track. Why Bhagwan chose this barren site, I don't know. Maybe he'd seen a few John Wayne movies and liked the sets, for this pure cowboy country. Every so often there are small outposts like ice-cream kiosks in which two *sannyasins*, man and maid, stand on guard in rosy garments. When they see us they smile and wave and shout joyous greetings as if we're St Bernards bringing in the booze. We pass a flower-decked grotto of the kind you find in the Pyrenees, except that instead of a

Madonna there is a picture of two flying birds, one black, one white, and the message:

> I go to the Feet of the Awakened One
> I go to the Commune of the Awakened One
> I go to the Ultimate Truth of the Awakened One . . .

The scenery is majestically desolate, the air suffocatingly pure. Orthodox America with its junk food, street gangs and edible panties seems light years away. We pass Krishnamurti lake and Gurdjieff dam. I ask a radiant youth in orange dungarees standing in a kiosk if there was water here before, how many people built the dam and where he comes from? The youth beams and replies in a broad Aussie accent, 'These are good and beautiful questions but I do not have time to answer you.' And he speaks rapidly into a headset, 'Silver Chevvy Suburban proceeding east from Checkpoint 11, registration number . . .'

We head into Rajneeshpuram, population 1,222, past bus stops, excavations, gigantic earth-moving equipment and groups of *sannyasins* who smile and wave so rapturously it reminds me of the early stages of the EST course I did back in '79 (you see I've been questing for *years*). When the crunch came, the EST people turned into tyrants. Will these orange-blossom fairies do the same?

We are directed to the reception centre, a tall airy building with wall mottoes such as: 'The Sage Does Not Talk. The Talented Ones Talk. The Stupid Ones Argue.'

A Stupid One, an elderly woman in lilac Crimplene, is arguing with reception about her hotel accommodation. The people next door, she complains, play music too loud, too late. So much for Serenity.

No, we say, we won't stay in the hotel. We'll take the A-frame cabin at $60 a day including three vegetarian meals, free laundry and transport and two meditation vouchers.

Are we, they ask, carrying explosives, guns or knives, and can they search our car for drugs? The drugs officer arrives, a not particularly joyful *sannyasin* in pink cords who fondles two of the receptionists absent-mindedly. 'Go on, Bear,' he commands a huge Alsatian, 'seek,' and Bear sniffs dutifully at our bags, pausing long and hard at wee Jim's Mothercare holdall. Is he getting high on zinc and castor oil?

There are two kinds of Rajneeshi. The ones who visit for a while and the communards who are permanent. These live-in *sannyasins* work twelve hours a day, seven days a week.

We go downtown to the collection of Wild West wooden shops and offices. There's a boutique with Gucci shoes, all pink and purple, and St Laurent jump suits, all orange and lilac. There's a gem store and a French restaurant. Instead of horses there are Rolls-Royces. Are they the famous Bhagwan Fleet of forty-seven? No, they're visitors' cars.

It's two o'clock. At this time every day the Master drives past. People hurry in from their work to stand by the roadside, their hands clasped in prayer. A truck comes first spraying the dusty road with water.

Next comes a jeep full of double-breasted heavies with a large machine gun mounted at the back.

And then a pale blue Roller with a small man in the driver's seat, a man with a woolly hat pulled over his head, a froth of grey beard, piercing blue eyes and an expression of such still sweetness it makes you catch your breath.

It is sunrise. We fall out of bed, pull on our red clothes and head for the early morning Dynamic, one of the two meditations included in our accommodation charge. As we jog down the dusty track past other cabins and larger dormitories, vaguely prurient thoughts about the sleeping arrangements of the live-in *sannyasins* cross my mind. There's a good deal of overt canoodling among the disciples, and this, together with the edict that 'in the interests of hygiene, condoms and rubber gloves should always be used', suggests that good times are just around the corner. Free buses, free minds, free love; it figures. I thought I'd be in good company bringing the baby, but James is a smash hit for the very good reason that he's the only baby in town. 'Oh please, *please* can I hold him?' was the constant cry from female *rajneeshi* whose maternal instincts had doubtless been subdued 'in the interests of hygiene'.

We cross a river and descend a flight of rocky steps to the gleaming white Hall of Meditation. We are late. Barefoot we pick our way through people dancing, eyes closed, to heavy metal sitar music. I am just beginning to get the hang of waltzing on the spot with my eyes shut without bumping into Mrs P, when the music changes to maximum decibel output and above the roar comes a strange high-pitched shrieking. My fellow Terpsichores are beating their chests, shouting 'Hup hup' and rolling on the ground. I modify my waltz to an up-tempo foxtrot, try shouting 'Hup hup' but I'm not convinced. Twenty minutes later we're back to dreamy temple bells and then it's over.

'How d'you feel?' I ask Mrs P as we head for breakfast.

'Exactly the same,' she says, and we both feel depressed.

Huge healthy breakfast packed with pulses, bran and fresh fruit. It's like any American college campus canteen, except everyone's wearing red. 'Will the Swami who borrowed a pen from the front desk please return it?' says the Public Address System.

'Where are you from?' I ask a pretty dark-haired girl.

'Bexhill,' she says.

'And what work do you do here?'

'We don't call it work. We call it worship. The places we worship in are called temples. I worship in the Finance Temple.'

Our guide for the morning is a ravishingly exotic girl from the Public Relations Temple called Ma Isabel, married to a Californian lawyer, also a *rajneeshi*, who worships in the

Rajneeshpuram Legal Temple. Isabel shows us some of the stupendous feats achieved by the city's inhabitants in just three years: the airport, with its fleet of aeroplanes; the market garden; the farm; the machine shop; the Re-cycling and Garbage Temples; the police station whose officers are called Peace Brothers. It's very impressive.

What's more impressive is the total contentment you see on everyone's face. I don't know the criteria for judging these things. My personal whiteness test is, 'Would I mind if one of my daughters went to live in Rajneeshpuram when she grows up?' The answer is no, I wouldn't. If she wanted to come she'd make out OK. As for the secrecy and brainwashing, parents of *sannyasins* can come any time they want and stay a week at the commune for free.

We stop for refreshments at the truck farm. The coordinator there looks like something from a James Bond film. She's wearing a Stetson, a pink bra top, teeny shorts and a walkie-talkie slung round her hips. I sit in the shade next to a wiry old lady with a face like a pickled walnut who asks in a broad Glasgow accent if I've had spiced tea. Her name is now Ma Diva or Ma Dipika but she was once Mrs Irene Reilly who became converted to Bhagwan ten years ago in her early sixties and has never been happier.

Driving back into town we pass a huge dumper truck. 'Hey,' says Isabel, 'you oughta meet Sibuti. He's English, used to be a journalist.'

'See you in the pizza parlour at eight,' says Sibuti. 'I'm on split shifts,' and roars away. We watch videos of Bhagwan teaching at his Poona Ashram. He's now apparently very ill and is always accompanied by an English nurse. If he were to die this minute, says Bhagwan, he would die content. He sounded almost wistful. My reporter training tells me to ask more questions about the Master. Where does he live, how much money does he have, who is the English nurse, why does he have forty-seven Rolls-Royces? But I can't. I believe he *is* an enlightened master, and such questions seem impertinent.

Eight o'clock in the pizzeria. Instead of a number you're given a card from the Tarot pack to tell you when your pizza is cooked. 'Awareness and Higher Consciousness, your pizzas are ready.'

Sibuti arrives. Ten years ago he was Peter Waight, political reporter of the *Birmingham Post*. Now he drives a belly dumper, shifts gravel and wears scarlet dungarees and a baseball cap. He does a lot of kissing and greeting when he comes in. I bet he couldn't do that on the *Birmingham Post*. We ask all sorts of questions. Is he happy, what happens if he isn't, what if he dislikes something or is late or wants to leave? Suddenly he stops smiling.

'Listen, I'm a little tired of these questions. They're irrelevant. This place is a goddam miracle and we built it with love. Excuse me, will you? I got a belly dumper waiting outside. I got work to do. We gotta city to build.' He called it a 'siddy'.

'Enlightenment,' calls the waitress. 'Enlightenment. Your mushroom and pepperoni is ready.' Enlightenment is my card. Looks as if this is the only way I'm going to get it.

We have been in Rajneeshpuram for three days, and my mouth aches from smiling. Not since the time I accompanied 200 student photographers (male) on a one-day course on a canal boat to learn how to take perfect Page Three pictures, have I been surrounded by such conspicuous bliss. It's the endless, ubiquitous, all-embracing (literally) bonhomie of the *sannyasins* that convinces me I couldn't live here permanently.

On Saturday morning Mrs P and I go to a star-shaped building called the Rajneesh International Meditation University to see if we can sign on for one of the individual spiritual development courses. There are dozens to choose from – Zencounter, Breath-energy-ecstasy, Dehypnotherapy, Neo-tarot, Neotantra, Sound and silence, Cleaning-up-the-past.

'Gee, I'd really like to help you guys but you're a little late,' says a cute little female *sannyasin* at the registration desk, flicking through a card index. I know it's frivolous and unworthy of me to think so but it reminds me of booking an appointment at Harrods' hairdressing salon except that instead of getting Michelle for a blow-dry, you get Swami Anand Teertha for a Body Celebration.

What's the Natarji session all about, we ask? 'Well, let's see now,' says Ma Pink Cutie. 'It's a totally blissful experience. I adore it but it does have just that little extra stretch' – she expands her hands graphically as if demonstrating the elasticity of a pantie girdle – 'but all our courses are designed to stretch you some.'

We sign on for Natarji and in the meantime I am persuaded to have a Rajneesh massage. 'What's so special about it?' I ask.

Ma Pink Cutie throws back her head and peals with silvery laughter, exposing perfectly crowned teeth. 'It's not an ordinary massage. The person who does it for you is like nobody else on earth, so your massage will be like no other massage on earth. I'll book you in with Ashika. Wow, Ashika is just *fantastic*.'

I pay my 40 dollars, and half-expecting a Michelle equivalent to help me into a pink floral cape and lead me to the shampoo, I'm disconcerted to see a tall, blond, besandalled *man* approach. 'Hi, Sue, I'm Ashika,' he says in a Swedish accent, and nervously I follow him to the treatment rooms. He closes the door, asks me to hang my dress up behind it and lie down. Gingerly prone on the massage table, my eyes tightly shut, I hear Ashika ask in smooth gentle tones, 'Is there anything you want to tell me about your body, Sue?'

'Like what?' I whisper miserably.

'Anything that will make me understand your body more.'

'Well, I had a baby four months ago, I'm short-sighted and I get this rash on my elbow when I'm nervous . . .'

'And are you nervous now, Sue?' asks Ashika.

'Of course not,' I whimper.

Ashika sighs, rubs scented oil on his palms and starts pummelling my left foot. It's nice, a lot nicer than the one I had in Swiss Cottage when I pulled a muscle, and as usual it makes me drowsy. I must have nodded off, for what seems like months later I awake to find my genuine Swedish masseur standing quite still beside me. 'Sue,' says Ashika, 'your body is in conflict with your mind.'

'Oh dear, is it? What shall I do?'

'Your body yearns to do things but your mind will not let it. Relax, Sue. Let go of your mind. Let your body speak to you, listen to your body. Let your mind submit to your body's desires. When I touch your body it responds, but always your mind says no.'

'I'll try, Ashika, I really will,' I say, struggling into my dress and buttoning up the wrong buttons. And I do. I let my body run all the way back to Mrs P as fast as it can and together we go to our next meditation, the totally blissful Natarji.

We are back in the huge empty space of the Hall of Meditation. There are only about a dozen of us. A small middle-aged woman with a Greek accent and a sweet, sad expression tells us what to do. We must dance for one hour without stopping and with our eyes closed so as not to break the chain of energy. Then we lie down for a while, then dance again to celebrate.

To start with I feel foolish, self-conscious, clumsy, but after a time I forget everything and just dance. When I lie down I find myself snivelling inexplicably, and when I dance for the last time I feel terrific.

Afterwards, the Greek lady teacher walks part of the way with us, and for the first time since coming to Rancho

Rajneesh I don't feel inhibited asking about our chances of finding enlightenment. It's probably because she isn't always grinning that we are so expansive. We know we need to develop and improve spiritually, we say, but we also know we don't fit in with happy commune life. We have kids and homes and jobs and husbands and we like junk food and planning holidays and being materially acquisitive, so is there any hope?

I won't tell you what she said because frankly I don't remember exactly. All I do know is that when we left Rancho Rajneesh I felt sad to be going. I wish I could fit in. It's no good though – lack of team spirit was one of my failings at school. The good news is that we met the chief coordinator of the English *rajneeshis* at the pizza parlour the night before. She said the Suffolk ashram is very English – cream teas, string vests, chamber music. I think I'm going to book myself in on a one-day course when I get back.